T0147809

TAKE YOUR SHOT, MAKE YOUR PLAY!

A COACH'S KEY TO FINDING SUCCESS ON AND OFF THE COURT

JOHN SAINTIGNON

TAKE YOUR SHOT, MAKE YOUR PLAY!
A COACH'S KEY TO FINDING SUCCESS ON AND OFF THE COURT

iUniverse books may be ordered through booksellers or by contacting:

iUniverse
1663 Liberty Drive
Bloomington, IN 47403
www.iuniverse.com
1-800-Authors (1-800-288-4677)

ISBN: 978-1-5320-4987-3 (sc)
ISBN: 978-1-5320-4986-6 (e)

Library of Congress Control Number: 2018907618

Print information available on the last page.

iUniverse rev. date: 07/31/2018

BOOK SUMMARY

Sports have always been the perfect metaphor for life. So often, we use sports and athletes as examples of the biggest ups and downs in life. Stories of athletes who persevere and end up taking the gold or winning the championship inspire all of us. "The thrill of victory and the agony of defeat" are words we all know well from sports but we all know apply to life too.

Take Your Shot, Make Your Play! is for students, athletes, coaches, entrepreneurs, salespeople, businesspeople, and anyone else looking for that edge that will get them to their goal or the top level of their career. The book is written by John Saintignon, one of the most accomplished basketball players ever to play the game at the NCAA level. Saintignon knows what it's like to play at the highest level and, more important, what it takes to succeed under a microscope. He not only won championships at all levels but also had the distinction of leading the entire nation in scoring one season. Saintignon went on to play professionally in Europe and Latin America. He also coached, taking his talents and his skills to the Middle East, Europe, South America, Latin America, and Asia. Now, Saintignon is an in-demand head coach and player development consultant who brings a great deal of experience and insight on what it takes to make it at all levels and in every field. He knows that lessons learned in sports and in coaching completely transfer to life and business.

In this book, Saintignon talks about his roots in the south side of Tucson, being adopted and raised by parents who never got past the eighth grade of formal schooling. Also, he shares his very personal journey from there to being on the court for some of the biggest games in the sport, as well as coaching in the Kingdom of Bahrain in the midst of the historical Arab Spring, with two young children and his wife with him.

But the book is much more than Saintignon's personal story; it is an inspirational book about the importance of setting high standards and not feeling afraid to take the shot and take chances. It is about learning from failure and the importance of credibility, overcoming obstacles, and making your wildest goals and dreams a reality. For businesspeople, players, coaches, and students, it also provides a straight look at what it takes to succeed and gives insight on how to go from wherever you are today to where you want to go.

THE MARKET

The primary and most obvious market for this book are the millions of athletes and coaches, from high school to college and professional leagues. But this book also perfectly suits businesspeople, salespeople, and other professional people. Both markets involve serious competition. They both require intense drive, risk, scrutiny, and preparation. And they both are extremely high stakes.

Readers of this book will include athletes, coaches, salespeople, business owners, and others around the world who all know that life, business, and sports are intertwined and that lessons from sports can make a big difference even to those who have never played in front of screaming fans.

THE AUTHOR

John Saintignon is the President and Owner of Orange County Magic Basketball, Inc. (www.ocmagic.org), an Amateur Athletic Union (AAU) basketball academy based in Southern California. He also teaches coaching and player clinics all over the world (www.johnsaintignon.com).

Saintignon played college basketball at the University of California–Santa Cruz, where he is still the all-time leading scorer. He also led the entire nation in scoring in 1985/86, when he averaged 31.2 points per game. He later transferred and graduated from the University of California–San Diego with a degree in economics. He also earned a master's degree from Liberty University in sports administration.

Saintignon is an accomplished coach. He won multiple championships at the high school level with different schools and went on to coach at Oregon State University and California State University Stanislaus. Later, he accepted the opportunity to coach professionally and internationally in Culiacan and Nogales, Mexico, and the Kingdom of Bahrain.

In addition to coaching, Saintignon has worked as an in-demand speaker, having gone to Italy, China, Poland, Croatia, Bahrain, Argentina, Colombia, Israel, Slovakia, Mexico, and the Dominican Republic to give insights into coaching and playing the game. He continues to give clinics in many places, including China, where he annually teaches the sport to hundreds of Chinese athletes. Also, Saintignon has published several articles and has a few videos on basketball and coaching.

AUTHOR'S NOTE

As a pro basketball player and coach, I share these stories with you to hopefully inspire you to pursue an extraordinary life. I would like to address you directly so you can perhaps see me as a coach. Please come along on this journey with me as we explore the concept of winning in life.

It Doesn't Matter Where You Begin, Only Where You Are Going

The year is 1983. I am a senior on the basketball team at Salpointe Catholic High School in Tucson, Arizona. We are playing a heated rival, Canyon del Oro, and it has come down to the final game of the season. We need a victory in order to get into the playoffs. It's a tie game; tensions are high. With seven seconds left on the clock, Coach Flannery, my animated and passionate head coach, calls a time-out.

During these lulls, it is typical of our coaching staff to have the junior varsity and freshman coaches present. Coaches Bob Scott and Chris Keeley are very calm and experienced. They give us players a sense of assurance since we have played for them both.

A play is drawn up. Seven seconds in a half-court setting gives you enough time to take about three dribbles before you have to shoot and the buzzer goes off.

John Saintignon

We take the ball out-of-bounds on our sideline, where my coach called the time-out. He has decided that we will inbound the ball to our point guard, at which point I must choose to come off either a single or double screen. We will set the single screen to the right of the floor, the double screen to the left. Because I shot the ball on the right side so many times as a child in my backyard, I feel confident in that area, so I choose the single screen to the right.

When the ball enters play, I flare to that side; I'm given the ball, and I dribble as hard as I can toward the right baseline and go into the shot. Two very tall defenders charge right at me. They look so long and athletic, their arms up in the air trying to block my shot, that I literally can't see the basket. I trust my instincts that I can make that one basket. The ball leaves my hands, and it feels so good, like the thousands of times I have shot baskets in my backyard. I don't see the ball go in, but I hear the horn blare. My coach and the rest of my team sprint out to me. We have won that game on the last-second shot, and we are on our way to the playoffs!

Any basketball player growing up during that period knew of Coach John Wooden of UCLA, arguably the greatest coach and basketball mind in the history of the sport. I was fortunate enough to have had the opportunity to work as a camp counselor at one of his basketball camps in Thousand Oaks, California, during my college career. I was so excited to take part in the teaching and learning process under Coach Wooden.

During the camp, expert guest speakers came through to talk to the hundreds of players, coaches, and counselors in attendance. One day, the expert guest speaker was a man named Luther Whitsitt, who was supposed to bring his two sons, Novian and Damon, to provide a supposedly legendary shooting demonstration. The sons could make all-net baskets at full speed with all-out intensity, rarely missing one. Everyone felt eager to witness these marvels.

Coach Whitsitt arrived with just one son, Novian, and therefore asked Coach Wooden if one of his camp counselors could join them in the demonstration. Coach Wooden looked around; sized up all the college basketball players in the room, who were also counselors; and chose me. Of course, I couldn't turn Coach Wooden down, so I walked onto the court and began to warm up. Right off, I felt an intense pressure and motivation to put the ball in the hoop. Looking over to Novian, I said to myself, *This guy doesn't hit rim? Then I can't hit rim either—nothing but net.*

Coach Whitsitt briefly described to the camp what was about to take place. He told us he and his boys began their training at five thirty every morning, working out in a high-intensity style and focusing on the discipline of making all-net baskets and on the concept of double and triple trajectory so the ball came down at a larger aperture of the rim. He described all this as he passed two balls around so quickly that we had no choice but to focus on the shot, realizing that every split second, another ball was coming at us.

I stood there and watched Novian shoot the ball so quickly, efficiently, and effortlessly and with such smooth intensity I immediately knew I had to mimic his pattern, while not falling on my face before my peers or Coach Wooden. I also understood that Coach Whitsitt didn't expect me to do the drill as well as his son, yet I was determined not to disappoint Coach Wooden for having selected me.

I was able to do the workout. I locked into what Coach Whitsitt was teaching me as I shot. It was a rare, unique honor for me to be selected to join them, and I cherished that. It would change the way I worked out from that point on in my career. I wanted to learn more.

We began by having two basketballs delivered to us to catch and shoot. This was intense, as Coach Whitsitt wanted us to make three baskets all net. Coach Whitsitt advised that I should just try to make the baskets, but what he didn't know was that I am driven by excellence and I wanted to make the baskets all net, just as Novian did, so I could stay in lockstep with the entire routine. We had a routine to follow, with the same principles of a very quick shot, another basketball being delivered thereafter, and, of course, the discipline of making the baskets all net.

I prepared mentally by allowing myself to be coached and relying on my strengths as a shooter. I stayed so concentrated on seeing the ball go through the net, trusting my form, having a proper trajectory, and maintaining intense focus as the next basketball would get passed to me. This allowed me to keep my concentration only on what I could control. It was at that moment that I experienced bliss, as previously, I had always been driven by seeing the ball go through the basket, but I had never before been driven to succeed in this manner, and I was loving it. I was being driven to my limits in front of hundreds of players and performing in a way I had not done before.

John Saintignon

It shocked Coach Whitsitt and Novian that I could do the workout with them without knowing their routine. Seeing me work out, Coach Whitsitt asked me if I really wanted to get better. He asked me if I wanted to train with him and his sons back in San Pedro. I jumped at the opportunity, as I wanted to get every edge that I could as a player and become the best I could be. I felt honored, to say the least, to receive this unique opportunity. The lessons that I learned with them helped me focus on becoming the best player I could be. Each season I increased my scoring in the NCAA, and eventually I was rewarded with the ability to play professionally. Such seemingly small events, which we all experience, can lead us down a path to an extraordinary life. The lessons I learned carried over into the rest of my life.

The very first step on the path to an amazing life is *deciding* you are ready. You must first make the decision to become the big shooter. This way, you will not look back on your life with regrets about what you could have done or might have become. In order to do this, you must discover what *motivates* you. What makes you jump out of bed in the morning and look forward to the day? For me, this is the game of basketball and all the challenges and thrills it entails.

Finding what motivates us isn't always easy. We often find things that motivate us for only short periods of time. But to fuel excellence, to fuel a life, we have to find *that thing* that will propel us throughout our whole life. Most of the time, early motivators come from people and things outside of us. And that's okay. Until we find that all-important inner drive or obsession, outside motivation is necessary and fine.

Here's a cliché: Life has many lessons. Yet, like most clichés, it is true! The vast majority of lessons come outside the classroom and outside traditional ways of learning. Most of the time, these lessons come from making the most of what life puts in front of us. We don't get to choose how things are—a game being tied, Coach Whitsitt arriving with only one son, Coach Wooden choosing me. These things happened beyond my control. However, each time, I did have a choice in how to respond to the opportunity or challenge placed before me.

I learned this lesson about choices many years back, for the two biggest choices ever made in my life were made for me—my being abandoned at a church as an infant and then getting adopted. Growing up in Tucson, Arizona, enjoying life as a kid in the neighborhood, I thought I was like the other kids in my working-class, largely Mexican neighborhood. As it turned out, I was and I wasn't. Unlike the rest of them, I was adopted and born not

4

in the United States but in Nuevo Casas Grandes, Chihuahua, Mexico. Go figure. My mom wasn't able to have children, so she adopted me and my sister before me. My mom asked her boss at the time, Mr. Hal Jones, who had lived in Chihuahua as a kid and still had family there, if he knew of anyone in Mexico who might be able to help her find a baby boy for adoption. Mr. Jones did find one—me—so my family drove to Chihuahua to pick me right up.

I was dropped off with the Mormons in Chihuahua, whom I remained with until I was four days old. Of course, I didn't know any of this for a number of years because my mom waited for the right time to tell me so I could properly process this information. And as expected, her own feelings were involved, and she probably thought that I would feel very strange— different—knowing about my first days. I think that this probably happens with a lot of adopted children. They wonder about and question a lot of things. *What happened?* I would ask myself after I found out. *Why did someone leave me and let me go?* I often thought about that too. I don't know what happened.

As I neared the end of my professional basketball career in 1992–1994, I found myself playing in Mexico. And lo and behold, we played in the city close to where I was adopted. But that road trip was so rigorous and I felt so exhausted I couldn't even muster up the energy to get out of my hotel room to go explore and try to get some answers to the questions about my family history. The life of a professional athlete involves so much physical work that when not playing or training, you, the pro athlete, sleep as much as possible to help the body recover. When you wake up, you have to get motivated to go out and perform. And then you're back out on the road somewhere else. In addition to the time crunch, part of me was reluctant to know the truth.

I was in sixth grade when my parents told me I was adopted. I could see the emotion that my mom was experiencing. Telling me really worried her. She struggled with how I would react and her own feelings. But I don't recall making a big deal about it or thinking much about it then. I just asked questions. I don't remember my questions having too much depth. It was later in life that I started to ponder a bit more and wonder about who my birth parents were. Whenever I was asked about my family's health history, I couldn't answer. I indeed wanted to know more, like why I was let go? Did I have any brothers or other sisters? What did my birth parents look like? I also wondered if they had ever looked me up to see what I had become. I'd love to go searching for those answers—but I have not gotten around to it. However, there is another side of it. If you pursue it, you risk opening up a sore spot for the birth parents too.

Finding out at the age I did (and finding out my sister was adopted at the same time) didn't overwhelm me. I stayed too active for it to do so. Being busy and active made it so I didn't focus on what this all really meant. When my parents told me about my being adopted, I responded, "That's great." But I didn't really know what being adopted meant. I just felt comfortable; I had people who cared for me and loved me.

Sure, I felt a bit different, knowing I was adopted. Everybody else had a parent. I had parents, of course—the people who raised me. But now, they weren't my natural parents. That little dilemma then started going back and forth in my mind. How would I identify myself? From time to time, I asked myself where I got certain traits from. I didn't know. But I was extremely fortunate because I could look at the other side and think about what my life would have been if I hadn't been adopted. For my natural parents to give me up, they must have had something serious going on.

Because I felt different, I wanted to be different in all that I did. I wanted to live my life without regrets and to have an extraordinary life. I used this dilemma as a pivotal moment to reflect on how I received each opportunity. We don't get to choose how life begins for us; we get to choose what we do with our lives. I was guided and influenced by everyone around me. I learned about the value of my education so that I could have choices in my life. You must decide to become extraordinary, regardless of how you begin your life.

My dad died when I was a freshman in college in 1983. I had come back during my college basketball break during Christmastime, and he suffered a heart attack and died. In that tragic moment, I was suddenly thrust into adulthood. Lots of things happened all of a sudden. People told me both good and bad stuff—not intentionally bad, but because I lived in an ethnic neighborhood, I kept hearing certain things: "Take care of your mom." "Of course, you're going to forgo school."

At the time, I was the only one in a good portion of the neighborhood going to a four-year university. It was even rarer that I played college basketball as well. I went to the University of California–Santa Cruz, majoring in economics, far away from the world I grew up in in Tucson, which was provincial in some of its thinking. So people asked me pointed questions, even at the funeral: "So you're going to move back and take care of your mom, right?"

Needless to say, I felt confused. I wanted to do the right thing. But the best thing my mom ever said to me was, "No way are you leaving school!" My parents made sacrifices for my and my sister's education. They sent us to private schools to get the best education possible. Mom was clear about school. "No, no, you're not staying here. You're going back to school and getting your degree and fulfilling your dreams!" That was wonderful on her part. She took the pressure off me.

But upon returning to my college campus after the break, a certain buzz surrounded me. Everyone, of course, discussed what they did over the holidays—parties, food, vacations. And there I was, saying, "My dad died." It gave me a weird feeling. I felt different. I was changed. I was on my own. I say to my two sons now, "No matter what you do in life, you'll need your father to help you get through certain things." But at eighteen, that was it; I was on my own. Fortunately, I had coaches; I had other people who guided me along the way. But in terms of having your own dad to rely on, I did not have that anymore. I was alone, figuring out life on my own. But I understand that a loss is a loss at any age.

My mom passed away in 2011. It was just her time, being older. Because she lived a long life, I obviously got to spend time with her all those years. We were very fortunate that I was able to return to Tucson to coach basketball, so she had the opportunity to spend a lot of time with my kids. It is the cycle of life.

I have so many things to recall from both of my parents. It was important to them that I follow my dreams. They always encouraged me even with things outside their norm. Who thinks their kid will want to play college basketball? They didn't know anything about that world. Yet they wanted to make sure I was educated enough to take care of everything. They fully supported me, which was great because when your parents are your number-one supporters, you feel confident. You can go out and do anything. After these life events, I felt driven to live my life without regrets, excel at whatever I chose to do, and pursue excellence.

My parents had a tremendous impact on how I approach life and coaching. My dad, for example, was constantly doing something, and I learned from him to not sit down. I constantly had to be doing something. To this day, I feel guilty if I am just sitting down. It doesn't feel right. It bothers my wife, and she often chides me to relax. But I always think of something else I should be doing. I got that industriousness from my father. My mom and dad also imposed on me the ultimate importance of an education. To this day, because of them, I put an emphasis on always learning, even beyond school.

My dad had a sixth-grade education; he learned about hard work and industriousness living on a farm in Ohio. He was always busy in the yard and fixing things around the house, and when he retired, he became even more involved in another business. He never slowed down. He would build worm beds, place them all over our backyard, and then sell the worms to bait shops or the rich soil to nurseries looking for that great type of soil. From him, I learned how to put two-by-four pieces of wood together to build a worm bed and then apply hinges to them so we could place a cover on them to protect the soil and the worms from the Arizona summer heat and sun. This took systematic care and attention. After we completed this, we then placed them on the ground and added the soil, along with the worms and fertilizer to help the worms while enriching the soil. We added compost as well, like eggshells and vegetables, for the worms to feed on. We also added water nearly three times per day to keep the soil moist. All of this taught me the value of doing hard work and having a routine, and taught me how to care for something.

My mom was a self-educated entrepreneur. She tried different things all the time. She had no fear of trying new things. My mom only reached the eighth grade. And that's why both parents so stressed education and ingrained in me a desire to learn. They were both right there for me.

When my mom helped with homework, she did the best she could. She tried to help but couldn't beyond a certain point in middle school. She was honest about it. One day, as I was in the eighth grade, we were doing math when she stopped, looked at me, and said, "I don't know how to help you anymore." But being the person she was, she decided she would get her GED while I was doing my own schooling. And she got it. I learned a lot from that.

Mom tried different ventures to keep income coming in and also keep busy. She did it all, from selling Avon products and BEE Line clothing, to working in insurance, to starting her own home- and office-cleaning service. It was remarkable. As a small-business owner, I know it's very difficult to think about everything involved in these ventures. Thinking about what she did back then, I am so amazed. My mom always inspires me.

While I was at university, Mom lived vicariously through me. She tried to understand what I was going through. Our phone calls consisted of her asking me what I was learning, trying to understand the material, and trying to get a sense of the classrooms, my roommates, and whom I was learning from. I remember when I received my bachelor's degree; she celebrated as if she had graduated. She went with me wherever I went; as I got awards or did anything, she was right there. It was special because I got to see how much that degree meant to her. I remember my college basketball coach giving me a bottle of champagne upon crossing the podium, and she took it, popped it, and drank from it. That whole night, she had that bottle of champagne with her. It was definitely her graduation too, the culmination of what she had sacrificed so much for. It was so wonderful to see.

Mom was my biggest cheerleader and supporter from the very beginning. I remember one time, she went to the starting gate of a big bicycle motocross race that I had when I was in grade school. She walked up to the starting gate at the top of the mountain at Randolph Park and whispered in my ear, "I think I can, I think I can!" She was my inspiration at the starting gate, my number-one fan. Another time, I remember her taking my dog to a basketball game. When I completed the eighth grade, my parents allowed me to get a puppy, so I did. His name was Conan, after the movie (and the book). He was a pit bull puppy, and I raised him and spent time with him daily. I wanted to train him to be special. I purchased a book on dog obedience training and did it myself. It felt fantastic to follow something and believe it would work out, especially when there was no prior reference for such a belief. Well, it turned out that I did it right and trained him properly.

One day, when Conan was still a puppy, my mom brought him to my basketball game at Salpointe Catholic High so that Conan could see me. She put him in her bowling bag, sat at the very top of the bleachers, and took him out and held him in her arms to see me play. It wasn't a secret for very long. Before I knew it, I could hear his little bark as he noticed me playing. During one of the breaks, I thought I heard my puppy and looked around, thinking I had lost my mind or was hearing something. I saw my mom, and she waved at me with a special grin that only a mom can give a son, with Conan's little eyes staring right at me.

It did not matter where I began. It mattered where I was going. I had people surrounding me who were going to show me each in their own unique way.

There Is a Razor-Thin Difference between Winning and Losing

In life, and especially in sports, you have a lot of teachers, a lot of people who influence you and end up playing a huge role in forming the person you later become. For me, that influence came from the coaches I spent a lot of time with when I wasn't at home with my parents. Many of them were like parents to me in their own way.

My first basketball coach, Fernando Fimbres, showed me the care and the fundamentals of the game with calmness and belief in me. He was the first to suggest to my parents that I had a special skill in the game and that it would be best if I went to a basketball camp and worked for it. Coach Fimbres taught me so much through traits he embodied without even speaking: patience, repetition, and calmness. He never overreacted or threw tantrums. He believed in me. Once our team knew the fundamentals and the repetition of what we did every day, he would hand over the reins at the games, as if to say, "You take it." We, as a team, learned how to handle ourselves by handling both winning and losing results the same way. We would feel devastated after a loss, but we had to shake hands with the victors, and Coach would downplay the disappointment.

Coach Fimbres encouraged us all to enjoy a new experience—a one-week summer basketball fundamentals camp in Prescott, Arizona, before eighth grade—which marked the first time any of us on the team left Tucson to play basketball. The team couldn't afford the camp, but we collected cans wherever we could—Kennedy Park, Rodeo Park, everywhere—to recycle them and earn enough money for the experience. Every Sunday, we would go out as a team to get the cans, because Saturday, everyone had gone out drinking. Our parents paid a little, and we were all able to go to the small and picturesque town of Prescott for basketball camp because our parents saw that we worked hard for it.

The camp's classroom style was intensive for us, and we had to take notes. It was awesome to see all the good players as well as the college coaches and excellent teachers of the game, all willing to help each player get better. I learned so much about respect, timeliness, attention to detail, and, of course, persistence with the game and the importance of continual improvement. As a result of that short but invaluable experience, I returned to Tucson for my eighth-grade season ready and prepared to help St. John's Catholic School win its first-ever Catholic Youth Organization (CYO) basketball title.

Another great teacher of mine was Carlos Serrano, who lived across the street from me in the Big House. Carlos was such an inspiration, with his drive, determination, and dedication to practice. He was the best motocross rider in the United States and practiced and rode harder and faster than others. I would go to the track to see him race and to see how he crushed his opponents, and then later, I saw him on TV, competing on *Wide World of Sports*—well, that was crazy. He embodied the south side, with his look, his swagger, and his confidence. He took care of the neighborhood.

I took my team to see Carlos years later when I was a high school coach and he was involved in NASCAR. He told them how the science of the turning was engineering and he had no degree in that; he just had the feel and the passion for what he needed to do as crew chief. The driver trusted his instincts as a competitive racer who had a feel for what needed to be done to win. I love that guy. He protected me several times during my youth. Once, when a dog bit me, Carlos told the owner that the dog had to be put down, as I had to receive plastic surgery as a consequence of getting bitten. Another time, when dealers were bringing cocaine into our neighborhood, he made it his mission to get them out of the neighborhood. And he did.

Another great influence on my life and coaching style was a guy named Virgil Banks. Virgil taught me to take risks and play up to the competition. For the first time, I felt that I had arrived on the basketball scene, as Virgil had played college basketball and had taken me under his wing to play all over the city. We went to different places, and he—someone who believed in me and carried himself with confidence—introduced me to the world of basketball outside my boundaries. He was like a big brother, helping me by being involved in the game, placing me in difficult situations to get me out of my comfort zone and to see players from all over with different skill sets. Usually, we played stronger and older players, which frustrated me at times, as I was not at their level yet, but I had Virgil's support to get out there and compete. And I always knew that he had my back and would protect me. Virgil taught me to trust someone to help me get where I wanted to go if he or she had already been there and wanted to help. It sounds simple, but a lot of young men don't always find it easy to trust others.

Coach Whitsitt was another great teacher. What I learned that day at the shooting demonstration changed my outlook. Coach Whitsitt told me he had never seen someone just walk into this type of situation and make baskets, and he asked me if I wanted to train along with his sons. Of course I wanted to! That marked the start of five-thirty workout sessions in San Pedro. I was staying in the Pasadena area at the time, thirty-three miles one way—a long drive.

The detail, the learning from failing, and the pressure of having to put the ball in the basket all net were incredible, while Novian and Damon watched to see if I could do it. I think it surprised them that I wanted to continue with this type of training and subject myself to what they had been doing since they were very young. I actually loved and craved the attention to detail. Coach Whitsitt pushed me and cared for me like a son, and his sons treated me like a brother. I went from averaging twenty points per game as a freshman in the NCAA, to averaging twenty-five points per game my second season, to leading the country in scoring thirty-one points per game as a junior because of the drive, attention to detail, sacrifice, and discipline I learned from Coach Whitsitt and his sons. It was a life-changing experience in many ways.

Basketball and the people in and around that world obviously played huge parts in who I would become and what I would experience in life. It still does to this day. But surprisingly, the person who has played the biggest role in my life had nothing to do with the sport when we met. I met my wife, Angelica, upon finishing my basketball career. I had decided I would retire from playing professional basketball, but I was not sure what I would do. I decided I would go to law school. I applied, and I was accepted in 1992. I returned to San Diego, having graduated from UC–San Diego. Fortunately, one of my friends, Sean Banks, was a resident assistant at one of the colleges in the University of California–San Diego system. He allowed me and another friend of ours, Isaac Williams, to stay there together. It was great. We got to stay on campus, a vibrant collegiate atmosphere, and I attended law school and studied with like-minded individuals.

Where we used to live, one of the floors had a study hall in an open room. It was always empty, so I used it as my place to open up all my books, spread out, and study. One day, in walked Angelica (unknown to me at the time). It shocked me because usually no one else was around. No one else had ever gone in there. So I said hello to her. And it petrified her because she didn't know me. I didn't know her either, but I found her a welcome relief because all I did was stress out from all the studying and the information I had to digest. There I was, an athlete, and now back in the books every single day. It was tough. It was misery. So that's how we started—just by saying hello. Then I kept seeing her come in. It was great. Then it went to the next level.

One day, I asked her, "Hey, do you want to go to a different library?" It gave me a way to get to know her a little bit better. This turned into library dates. It kept progressing from there, from library dates and talking to hanging out more and more. We became closer and closer. In 2018, we will have been married twenty-one years. And we were together five years before that. I met her at a time when I was looking for someone to bring joy to my life—someone with a different outlook. While I struggled to figure out what I wanted to be in life, she was there and willing to stay by my side. She also encouraged me to follow my passion.

Here's where my dad's influence came into it as well. He told me long before those days with Angelica that I would have to talk to my prospective mate about three things. "One is that basketball will be in your life somehow, some way; you don't know how. But she has to know it, understand that, and appreciate it. Whether that's you watching basketball on television or you playing, basketball will be a huge part of you. She doesn't have to love it the way you do, but she can't be anti-basketball either. Two," he said, "you'll need someone who can take care of things while you are not around. And three," he advised, "she'll need to be someone you can have intelligent discussions with about meaningful subjects—maybe one day having and raising children, buying a house, and having jobs and careers. And if you're not around," he added, "you'll want to know she's intelligent enough to take care of things."

I've never forgotten that coming from him. And I do remember one time after Angelica and I had grown closer, she and I were on a swing at a park, near my sister's house, and those questions started to come out of me. "You know, basketball is going to be in my life. You okay with that?" She was on board and willing to take a risk by being with me and proceeding in life together. And so, I found myself driving to go get a ring, and I couldn't imagine what I was doing, almost as if I was on autopilot.

I wanted to be as traditional and respectful as I possibly could, so I drove up to her parents' house to ask her father for her hand in marriage before I asked her. I sat with her father. He was not sure what I wanted to talk to him about. Once I got to his house, I told him that I wanted to get his approval for his daughter's hand in marriage. He and I sat there, and he asked me question after question. And I answered them all. In the end, I was relieved to get his blessing. The next thing I knew, I proposed to her on Valentine's Day. That was the start of our whole love affair.

The marriage has had its ups and downs, like any other relationship and any other marriage. It's so carefree at the beginning, but then, life steps in—mortgages, jobs, moves, births, and child-rearing. But through it all, she stood by my side, and she's still there. I'm very fortunate that wherever I have gone in the world, she has always wanted to come with me, even going out of the country for coaching jobs. A lot of people have asked her, "You're going to move?" as if moving is a bad thing. Moving allows you to see different things, to experience different parts of the country and different parts of the world. Fortunately, she has that same mind-set.

We now have one son in college and another son who is in high school. They have already experienced the world in ways most people much older than them have not. Their passports have been stamped numerous times already. They can speak a smattering of languages, and they know and appreciate different cultures and religions. They have benefited greatly from my wife and I moving and being willing to take risks and move out of our comfort zones. The risks have paid off in ways that even we did not expect. That is one of the benefits of being a risk-taker; often, you get far more than you planned for.

One thing that led to my confidence to take risks was the education I had and the fact that I graduated with the mind-set that I had the power to do whatever I wanted to do. I had choices in life, instead of being told what to do. With that mind-set, I decided to follow my passion, thinking if I did what I felt passionate about, I wouldn't consider it work. Initially, I think I chased money because my mom thought college was all about that. So I chose economics as my major in college because it involved money and finance. I felt miserable because I was doing what I thought I was supposed to do, not what I really wanted to do. I should have majored in sociology because I love to study people and habits. But I pushed through to that economics degree and got it despite having many trials and tribulations with my classes on my way to earning my degree.

One day after I had retired from playing professionally (already having decided I didn't want to pursue a career in law), I got a call from Coach Mark Aumann, my former assistant coach at UCSD, about an open high school coaching position that he thought I would be great for. I applied, even though I didn't know if I could transfer my knowledge as a player to someone else. I interviewed, and I got the job.

We struggled at first as a team. The players just lacked the playing skills and understanding of the game as it pertained to playing with each other. As a coaching staff, we changed how we practiced and decided it was more important to have them see how Coach Isaac and I played together and how we read and reacted to each other. Our players then got to play against each other in two-on-two and three-on-three settings, getting a chance to learn from each other and see the game develop in front of them. We finished the first year at .500. We finished on a ten-game winning streak, so in some ways, we had a phenomenal start. And then the next year, we were really good, ranked as high as sixth in the state. By then, I'd started to figure things out, developing a philosophy and technique along the way as well. I was having a blast yet not making a lot of money. It made me fully realize that joy really isn't about the pursuit of money. It is about having passion and joy every day. It is about influencing lives in ways I never thought I could. From there, I stayed in high school basketball and kept moving up the ladder, on to things and places that I had never even dreamed about. And all the joys and successes came about all because I didn't try to chase money as my happiness.

From being adopted from Mexico to seeing the world and influencing lives through a sport, life has given me plenty of lessons and opportunities. I am glad I was raised to have the courage to pursue any and all opportunities. In doing so, I was encouraged to find that inner motivator in my life. And that motivation became ever clearer to me. Finding myself in a position to take that last-second shot in high school meant hours and hours of work and practice.

But I had found my passion, so it wasn't work to me. It was joy. I found the passion to do exactly what all the moments up to that shot had prepared me for. Each of us has something like that in us. We just have to find it.

Decide you are ready to become extraordinary. Make the decision to be different. Discover what inspires you. What moves you? Who is on the journey with you to help you succeed? Many people all around you are there to help you. Once you know that, your journey to greatness begins. It's time to take your shot and to make your play.

The Devil Is in the Details

It's the 2012 season, and I am a professional basketball coach in Mexico. This league has heated rivalries. In this particular league, teams play four times a week and very intensely. In this particular game, we are losing badly to a team called Cananea. A series of events need to happen if we are going to win the game. We're losing control because it is intense at their place, a very small box gym, which is very difficult to travel to—lots of twisting, winding roads. At this time of the season, it gets very cold, dusty, and dirty. And it is very unfriendly every time we show up. No one here wants to lose to a rival.

When we entered the building, we had to go into a place and change where there is water everywhere on the floor. The atmosphere is horrific. The locker room is not pleasant, and neither are the people. We prepare to play in the basement. As soon as we got onto the floor to warm up, lot of hatred got leveled at us simply because of the city we're in and playing. One lady sitting directly behind me, dressed in purple, totally berates me with expletives of all sorts. Of course, she doesn't know me; it's because I coach the other team. It all adds to this environment of heated moments. Because its home court for the other team, they are on fire. It is a tough atmosphere.

In professional basketball, there is a twenty-four-second shot clock. We have three imports on the team—three Americans. And if any of them gets into foul trouble, I have to rely on the bench for "domestic" help, and perhaps the American on the other team will take advantage of that and score because maybe that player is just a little more talented. And that is the case. We experience foul trouble because emotions are high. A lot of things fall beyond your control when you play this game of basketball.

You get multiple time-outs per game, and I decide I will use them at every opportunity, in addition to the television time-outs. TV time-outs come every four minutes, but I dictate the action. Every time I see a six-point swing, I call a time-out to stop momentum. Or I change the substitute pattern so I can stop the other team's momentum. In the game of basketball, teams go on runs where they play unbelievably well. I try to get that across to our team. There's a cycle.

The momentum is in the other team's favor, but I try to stop that momentum. We need to use the shot clock to ensure that we control momentum and we can get a great shot. I want a great shot—not a good shot, a great shot. I start to say to my team, "It's just us here." My General Manager, Aleks Martinez, is there, sitting on the bench with us. He goes on the road with us. I decide that we will enter the ball on one side of the floor and pass it to the other side of the floor after a series of cuts so that I can get the defense to shift and see how they will defend for a longer series on defense. I want a systematic approach that we can execute consistently. I am even willing to take a shot clock violation, because as a coach in the PAC-10 Conference, I learned a shot clock violation is sometimes a good thing. At least it would give us five players back on defense and make sure we don't do some desperation shot, which could lead to an odd-number break, like three-on-two or two-on-one, which usually leads to a certain basket for the other team.

My players then get locked in because it is just us, in an us-against-the-world type of scenario. We end up cutting into the lead and getting it close. We then tie the game. We know now that we have secured the momentum for us. We put pressure on the other team now to make baskets, with their being at home adding pressure. And they don't. They miss. At this point, it is all us as we start to execute. We force them to play a longer series of defense than they want, which leads to us getting the ball where we need to get it. We control our own destiny.

We end up winning the game. It feels gratifying and special because it has been years since Nogales has beaten Cananea on their court.

Once you have decided the extraordinary life is for you, how do you go about constructing this life? Plenty of people dream of success and greatness, yet *how* does one actually manifest this hope or intention? By paying attention to detail, by preparing, and by having a plan.

Coach Wooden would always say there is a fine line between winning and losing. The line always comes down to the process that teams and people go through to get to the end. It is always about focusing on all the little details and not just the big, obvious final outcome. In terms of basketball, for example, it's about how many possessions you have in the game and what you do with those possessions. You have to take care of that ball, the possession, and you have to get the best possible shot that you can. It's in the little details that you win or lose because those little details end up becoming big things at the end. Most times in basketball and sports, people look at what's magnified at the very end of a game. But that's not necessarily most important. What's important is all the movement and work up to that.

The margin between winning and losing the 2016 NCAA Tournament between North Carolina and Villanova was one final shot. That one shot lives in eternity. But that's the fine line between winning and losing. As a coach, you go back and review those possessions. I can count a handful of possessions North Carolina had that they'd like to get back because they threw the basketball away. They lost the possession. But here's the thing; you can't get it back. You have to go get it some other way in some other form or fashion.

It's the same in business and relationships. Our processes are at stake. How do we take care of the little things so that we have success at the very end? The way I plan a game is all about our team's preparation, and then ultimately achieving what I intend for them. I work my way from the finish line backward. What do I anticipate success looking like? Now, let's go backward and figure out how that will happen. So much goes into winning a contract, winning a game, or winning at all. It comes down to those little details that you might take for granted, which could become big issues at the end.

John Saintignon

As a player myself, I led the country in scoring in the 1985/86 season. I paid attention to every single detail so that I would have an edge. My personal approach was to wake up before anyone else. At five thirty every morning, I was already on the court, whether inside a gym or outside on a concrete court. I wanted to not just make baskets but make them at full speed and without touching the rim. I wanted to have the ability to train three times per day and go one-on-one full court so that I could learn the truth about myself.

I had to make my conditioning an advantage, as, at five foot eleven, I was not very tall. When I attended Five-Star Basketball Camp as a high school player, it opened my eyes to the rest of the players in the country who were so talented—more so than I was. I returned to Tucson with an attitude that no one would outwork me. This attitude wasn't for everyone. But it was for me, as I was driven by the details. I later transferred my personal approach to my coaching approach.

In the system that I currently coach, we must have all five players on the same page, working together to help one another succeed. We must communicate both verbally and nonverbally. We train every day in a game called *seven*, where we get used to various situations that present themselves during games. There is a game within the game, as I call it, and we must learn how to manage every two minutes. In this game, I award one point for a basket made inside the key, two points for a shot made outside the key before the three-point line, and three points for a three-point basket. If I call a foul, it's one point for the team, but the ball goes the other way.

If the game is tied at 4–4, I want one of the teams to go for the win, because if they miss, they will foul to get the ball back and have another shot at it. When one team reaches six points, there is a two-fouls-to-give rule in place. This means that if the team fouls, it counts as only the foul, no point; the team keeps the ball and has another chance. This is where execution becomes critical. All the little details come into play. Communication has to happen on both ends as the offense and defense try to exercise their will over the other to get the win.

In 1999, when I was head coach at Bonita Vista High School in Chula Vista, California, we had to go through one of the traditional powerhouses in basketball, Torrey Pines High School, in our playoff run to get to the final California Interscholastic Federation (CIF) game. I reminded the players of our two-minute drill. Each one of them knew what I was talking about. It had come time to concentrate all our efforts on our possessions to focus on getting to seven points first. Our players paid such attention to detail and had such focus that it became our mantra during each time-out in that fourth quarter. We advanced due to this attention to detail and earned the right to play in the CIF final game, where we won the school's first-ever CIF championship in basketball.

Each game has a game within the game, and as a coach, I can only stop it a few times with a time-out to help stop the other team's momentum or help our team's players get rest in substitution patterns. This is a process to use, but really, it's up to the players out on the floor to think the game through and play through the two minutes of each game. If I can train my players to think the situation through, they stay engaged in what happens, know what they have to do to play to win, and get to the seven points. During our games, you will hear a score shouted from the sidelines to remind those on the floor of the game's score and remind them what is needed—to make a good stop, to go for the win with no fear, or to defend with purpose and shoot the ball with confidence.

The 2016 NCAA Championship is a perfect example. Villanova controlled what they wanted. And they lived with it. They understood who they were. Part of our winning and losing process involves knowing who we are and not trying to be someone we're not. I think so many coaches and businesspeople look to others for a way to act but don't really know who they are themselves. A lot of times, I look at young coaches who seem so clouded by what they see on television, and they want to emulate that. You can do a lot of the things you see on television, and you can implement them. But can you really teach them effectively? Do you know their intricacies? It's the same in business. People copy products and business models. But do you know the product? Do you know that way of operating? A lot of details go into that original product or practice the copy might be missing. Have you tried too much to copy someone else?

For example, with our AAU program, Orange County Magic Basketball, my business partner, Coach Sean Sargeant, and I have an idea that we know works for us. There are so many other ways to do things—lots of ways, actually. But I know what works for me based on the successes and failures I've had in my life and career. I know if I do too much, I will not be effective. If I can focus on those small details, especially in a practice setting, I can definitely be more effective. I see so many coaches go into a practice with so many things to accomplish that they end up accomplishing nothing. The focus just isn't there.

John Saintignon

Every day, I tell our team's players what our practice should look like at the end. Before I even begin, I lay it out so they get a clear picture of what I anticipate. I tell them we will learn from failure, and we will learn from winning and losing, but they will learn so much more from losing because that failure will stick in their mind and come back in ways that lead to future successes. I want players in our program to know that basketball is a tool to get an education and we will prepare them to give their best effort and have awareness of how to act, look, and respond to any and all situations. We, as coaches, will be aware of the little details and take care of things that we can, like acting with class whether we win or lose, and remember to teach those under our supervision to have joy and passion for the game and to use this time in their life to play with a purpose.

I think a lot of people are driven by pain or pleasure. One of those two principles guides you. If you ask a person out on a date, you will experience the pleasure of that person saying yes or the pain of hearing no. What primarily motivates you to take that risk? Do you focus more on the potential pleasure or the potential pain? That's why some will take the shot, or ask, and some will not even try. It depends on whether pleasure or pain is the greater motivation. One or the other will motivate you.

When you ask people, especially in the coaching profession, what they remember most, they'll tell you they remember the losses most. That's because they look to see what they can correct, what they can do better. I remember talking to Coach Wooden, and he would say he knew when the players' effort wasn't great even when they won a game because they had the greater talent. Despite their talent, he still had to find a way to motivate them to get better. So he started to define his players' *success* not by their winning but by their playing to the best of their ability and their effort. That transformed the way UCLA approached everything. They no longer approached the game in terms of wins and losses; they measured whether they lived up to their capabilities. So he altered the process.

Angelica and I, as parents of two boys, want our sons' best effort. It isn't the final degree that matters, or the final grade; it is their effort. Do they give their best effort and retain their knowledge on a daily and weekly basis? I've had teams where we've lost and I've considered it a huge success because we played to the best of our ability. The effort that we gave based on the talent level that we had made me so happy.

What is the difference between winning and losing? It's that self-satisfaction that you've given the best effort you possibly could. The public defines *success* by the end result; did you win? But that's not what *success* means in reality. The 2016 NCAA Championship will go down as one of the greatest college basketball games of all time, and people will forever remember that final shot. But really, possession after possession was what mattered in the end. When Villanova threw the ball away, the tension in the stands was palpable. But for the players and coaches on the court, it was about the next play, the next detail, the next assignment. When those mistakes happened, Villanova's coach told them that the only thing they could control was their attitude. That was their mantra all year long. Players would join the huddle and remind each other that the only thing they could control in that particular moment was their attitude.

I always say to my teams, "It's next play." This comes from my shooter's mentality. If I missed, I knew that I had to play defense, but I knew after that, my next shot would go in. I learned from it in that instance, as the next time I took a shot, I had to make a decision based on my last result. As a coach, I teach players to learn from the shot; learn from what happened, but move to the next play, make or miss. We don't have time to pout or put our heads down. "It's next play!" Let's not make the same mistake twice; let's learn from that one. This outlook applies to relationships, business, and all kinds of things we do.

We've all made mistakes. We can feel bad about those mistakes, and we can then make the same mistakes again. We'll keep on losing until we learn from those mistakes. It really is a fine line. Usually, the little things add up to the big thing in the end. The same concept holds true with athletes; all the little things that you focus on and improve will come back, and when you put them together, you look like a great basketball team.

A basketball game is like a classroom test; you go to school to learn what you need to know to succeed on it. A teacher made this same point to me. You need energy and excitement as a teacher in the classroom. You also need to change things up. You can do the same things, but with a slight change here and there. When you walk into my practices, you'll see I try to be energetic. I call out nicknames. I try to intrinsically motivate players through their passion for the game. I need to bring it out; I need them to feel comfortable and to understand that it's okay for them to make noise.

The little things I do every day include shaking hands with every player and asking them all how they're doing. I don't even bring up basketball. I try to get them laughing, to find something they enjoy, and to see how they feel, because how they feel is a big part of how they will do in practice. Then we go through whatever our routine will be that day. And here's the thing I know and accept: absolutely nobody gives 100 percent all the time. There's no such thing, really. Sometimes, we only have 60 percent and all I ask is they give all that 60 percent they have that day. That's what we're trying to accomplish—to push that out. Now, how do we go about doing that? The little things bring that out. It's about focus.

You could do a passing drill and focus on their fingers. Do they point? For example. You can make it fun. That's what master teachers try to get at. They do the same drills that everybody else does, but they change the focus so the athletes or the students feel something different. In terms of shooting, for example, there are the basics involved, like balance, eyes on target, elbow position, and follow-through. But I might instead concentrate on players' feet and their separation, and then, once they've mastered that, we can focus on scoring, competing against the clock, and seeing how many baskets we can make. But at first, other things are our focus. Every single drill might be universally the same in practices coast to coast, but I change the focus in my gym. One day, the focus is on the ball not hitting the rim. Even though the focus is completely different, the players zero in on it. They lock in with these changes. That's the challenge every day—finding that change of focus that keeps practice fun and motivating.

In your own line of work, you will have the same routine every day in some ways. But how will you find ways to make the routine fun—to accomplish it without having to painfully drive the work out of you? My players and I go about our business every day in a systematic way, but I want them to have curiosity and wonder a bit about what each day will bring. We might concentrate on half court, three players on four players, mismatches, or restrictions, like having only four dribbles. Those little things completely change their view and focus.

That need for fun applies to every industry. As a salesperson, how will you make your cold call? You could make it with a smile. You could start laughing before you make that call to make the call feel more welcoming. I want players to leave the building happy at the end of the day; I learned that from one of the companies I worked for when I was younger. We ended every meeting by pounding on a conference table and saying something motivational and loud. The first time I did it, I confusedly looked around the office building as we pounded on the conference table. But when I saw the passion the other employees showed when doing this, I found their passion contagious. This behavior was different; it was unique. It led to smiles and renewed everyone's energy.

As a basketball coach, I've always had our team's players come together and sing and dance at the end of practice, and then, I have everybody say goodbye to each other. And almost without fail, after that, they don't leave the building right away. They end up hanging around, smiling, shooting on their own, and enjoying each other. This includes my professional athletes, who played four times a week, were often tired, and sometimes came in cranky. At the end of practice, they would leave the building happy. Because of the fun we have, the players come back the next day with a great attitude, eagerness, and curiosity, asking, "What's new? What's going to happen today?" They know we have only so much to cover. There's offense, defense, and only so much basic stuff. But we can cover those things in new ways; we can cover them by facing new challenges. And I can put the players in different and difficult situations and see how they learn and achieve success out of those.

In business, you ask what you can do differently to motivate your employees or to help employees motivate themselves. For example, we've seen a big cultural shift in businesses from a suit-and-tie corporate setting to a relaxed corporate setting. You see a lot of companies that no longer keep track of your time; they only care that the work gets done. They even have exercise classes, short nap times at work, and things like that. You can hold staff meetings in a different way too. You have to think outside the box for your employees. You must have new and innovative ways to keep them interested in doing different and difficult work. They are no different from athletes. They all want to succeed. But how do you get there?

If business owners looked from the finish line backward, paid attention to all the details required to get there, and came up with a unique and fun approach to reach it, they would find it fosters employees who are intrinsically motivated and not just about the money. In my professional coaching career, if I had a professional basketball player who was only motivated by money, I knew the player's career would likely be short-lived. You must have a better motivator. Finding that drive and that intrinsic motivation is what matters.

So what is *drive*? Drive is creative. Google, for example, completely changed things and encouraged employees' drive when they set up their culture that encourages employees to stop their tasks and spend a dedicated part of their day doing nothing but thinking freely to be creative. Well, what came out of all that drive and creativity were Gmail and Google Hangouts, and many other unbelievable things. This approach has led to revolutionary outcomes because it takes that passion, that drive, and employees' brains and creativity to come up with new and exciting ways to do things and stay motivated.

Look at Steve Jobs of Apple. Look at what he created and accomplished. He changed the world with his products. But money didn't motivate him. His creations motivated him; he wanted them to be revolutionary. Money came as a by-product of that. One of the great stories about him involves when he took over in Silicon Valley. He put a skull and crossbones on a flag and raised it up a flagpole on top of Apple's headquarters. Apple took no prisoners. They went after the industry. But they were nobody at the time. Do you think that inspired the employees (there were only ten of them at the time)? You bet it did. It inspired them to get creative, to do whatever they had to do. Then products started to come out of Apple. They started to think differently, to just try stuff. Did they have failures? Of course. They had failure everywhere, but they kept learning from it.

NASA is another example of a place that has promoted drive and innovation. How many failures has NASA had in trying to get a spaceship off the ground? But out of those failures have come some incredible moments of progress in our history.

Some people don't know how to bounce back from failure. They let failure or a slump define them or cause them to go further and further into darkness. But people have to remember that everybody fails sometimes. The key is getting over it and trying again, accepting that failure is part of the learning process. Every one of us failed at learning to walk at first. We fell down on our first tries. But we got back up and learned from it without being told how. But at some point, unfortunately, we learned that losing and failure are bad. We do have businesspeople and coaches who dwell on losses and want to make you feel bad about them, especially in professional sports. In the professional world, you lose a game, and you really have to hear about it. People want to talk about it, boo you, write about it, and talk about it on the radio and television. They discuss it constantly. But fortunately, by the time you become a professional athlete, you've probably learned to think about the next play and developed a thick skin.

When you find yourself in that negativity, I think you sometimes have to partner with someone who has found success and who can show you a different manner, a different way. That requires a lack of selfishness. I know that in all these businesses and sports, selfishness exists. Many companies have a high achiever who makes many sales and does very well when the rest do not, and therefore, the rest feel like failures. I believe a manager or CEO should look to pair the high achiever up with another salesperson, maybe even have them go out on sales calls together. Inevitably, it will become clear that their discrepancy in success is about the enthusiasm that one has versus the other, the negative self-talk that one has versus the other. When I notice an athlete of mine who lacks positivity, I tell him to listen to positive, happy music. I show the athlete YouTube clips that can bring him up and inspire him to believe he can take on a challenge and stay positive. The world is full of underachievers who became overachievers. David and Goliath stories of people overcoming obstacles and achieving success are not unusual at all.

We all want mentors and guidance. For example, I read constantly about others' experiences and learn from their wisdom. I am in my fifties, and I'm still looking for that lesson, that edge, from someone who has already achieved success. I still try to challenge myself to think about things differently, or at least reaffirm what I already know.

To motivate others as a coach or leader in any capacity, you have to know people beyond their skills. Coach Wooden told me that nobody cares about what you know until he or she knows that you care. It was a simple but true lesson. You think you have a lot to share, but people don't care—not until they know you care about them. Then they will listen to everything you have to say. So what form does showing you care come in? It comes in the form of a handshake; it comes in the form of asking personal questions: "How's your wife? How are your kids?" To ask this, you must know if they have kids. It's the little things. Go back to the little details. Know about things in their lives outside the company or the gym.

For all professional basketball players, life on the road can feel lonely. As an athlete, always on the road, you never feel that you can let your guard down in public. For this reason, when I coached professional players, I would have them at my house every Sunday. My wife would cook like crazy for all of them, and we'd hang out and not talk about basketball. On those Sundays, I couldn't have cared less about basketball; I just cared about us being together. We first did this when I was a high school coach and a coach in the NCAA. Eventually, the players would play board games together; Pictionary was a favorite, as it put our players onto teams. Some unique bonding took place, when the players let their guards down, laughed, and poked fun at each other's drawings. It was the best time, and it reinforced trust, communication, and a sense of togetherness. Sometimes during tough moments, I would use one of the drawings to lighten the mood, change our thinking, and provide enjoyment.

Details. Little details. That's the difference between winning and losing. By the time that final shot swishes through the net at the end of a game, you've dealt with a whole lot of unseen details that made that moment possible. Always focus on the details. It's not enough to be passionate. You have to be smart too.

Confidence Is the Secret Ingredient

Mar Vista High School in Imperial Beach, California, is where I first got my start as a head coach. It is the southwesternmost school in the United States, near the border of Mexico. It was a forgotten school in terms of enrollment, identity, and location. The basketball team had not won a league title for more than thirty years. It was a program in disarray—unkempt floor, no basketballs, not enough uniforms, no attendance, not even players who wanted to come out to join the team, just a complete lack of pride. I had to instill a belief in me and also immediately instill a new positive culture. It helped that the players could identify with me because they could see I was willing to do everything I could to help them believe we could achieve what I suggested. This trust helped get the players' complete buy-in so they were willing to follow what my fellow coaches and I laid out in front of them and to believe in what we told them.

No greater challenge came to our program than one we faced in year two of my tenure, when we had the opportunity to play against a private Catholic powerhouse in San Diego, St. Augustine High School. The reason they were so powerful was they had an unbelievable roster of athletes, led by two in particular. One had returned from the Nike All-American Camp, where he was considered one of the most sought-after players in the country (eventually signing with UCLA and having a professional career). The second player was six foot five and ended up playing football for USC as well as having a career in the NFL. We had to carefully prepare for that—our single greatest challenge—as the tallest player we had that year was a six-foot-five guard who had transferred in that season. The rest of our team was very short and small, but we had a spirit among us. We would always compete.

We entered the week of practice leading up to the game with my coaches holding brooms to simulate the height of one of the tall opposing players. I had the coaches push our players over and over in the post to simulate the opposition pushing them. Our game plan was to do what we did best: run and let our home crowd feed us with their energy, get on every loose ball, show no fear, and get one time to take it to them. If we had a chance to dunk the ball on them, we would do it. We would never show it if we felt intimidated.

Our main catalyst to begin the game off right was our super-athletic, six-foot-five dunking machine, Sidney Faison, who, the first chance he got, went right at the tallest guy on the other team and dunked the ball with something so ferocious that our crowd went crazy! He was the key to our week of practice, as he showed he believed in us as coaches. The rest of the team believed in us too. Our message was clear; we would do what we did and let the chips fall where they may.

The fever pitch in our gym was so intense that we remained poised during the whole game, even when St. Augustine tossed our smaller post players all over the floor. Our players showed that they believed in what we had laid out for them. They trusted that I had been there before as a player and that, as a coach, I would lead them. We stood firm with our game plan throughout the game and pushed every opportunity. Make or miss, we sprinted to see whether those big bodies could stay with us, as we hoped to create a five-on-four situation. We got into a pace and style of game that benefited us. We neutralized as best we could our size mismatch with our speed.

Ultimately, we won the game, scoring in the mideighties. We had such a celebration on the court with the fans rushing the court to join in. It was very memorable, as it was our gym's first sellout game in recent memory, and we pulled off an upset as a team and a school that virtually no one had ever heard of before. Our players, administration, fans, student body, family, and coaches all found it so gratifying.

You have no chance for success with a team, a customer, or any situation without first getting buyin regarding your credibility. Without it, no one will listen to you, follow you, or buy what you are selling, whether it is a philosophy, a product, or a supposed expertise. Credibility comes in a number of forms and fashions. Coaches, for example, trust people who have been through the fire and the ups and downs as credible. With players, they have to surrender their ego. They have to be open to being taught.

But how do you establish this commitment? Players have their defenses built up already. How will they let go of those? Ultimately, the key is they have to trust that what I say to them will make an impact on them and help them become more successful. They can also develop this trust by seeing the success of others I have coached.

From my first impression, I tell an athlete who is going to work with me, "Hey, no flip-flops, no shoes untied, shirt tucked in. Look people in the eye, arrive early, and then we begin our business." That's my way. I teach players, "You have to be concerned about your appearance." I want to teach them how they can make themselves exude credibility before they even get started on basketball. But this guidance has to make sense to them. They have to relate to it. Guidance on taking pride in one's appearance starts from an earlier age, with teaching little ones how to shake hands. Credibility even comes in from that act of a proper, confident handshake. How you greet customers at the door, how you take orders over the phone—you name it, credibility comes in so many forms.

But credibility, of course, is about so much more than how you look and how you shake hands, though those are critical components of credibility. As athletes move up the levels, before they commit, they want to know if you know what you are talking about, if what you say has a proven impact, and if what you say applies to them. For example, when you call someone with a question and he or she can't answer it, it can leave doubt in your head; it's the same with players. If you can't answer their questions, they'll have doubts about you, and they'll do their own thing. Players always ask why. They always want to know why. When athletes are younger, they don't necessarily ask why; they just do what you say. Around the world, I always tell coaches to understand what they do and why they do it, because eventually, they will come across an older, experienced athlete who will ask them why they want him to do something. What's its purpose and credibility?

Everything that I do in my clinics has a why attached to it. Coaches do a lot of things that are routine. They have players dribble all over the place around cones and chairs, and it looks like busywork. Why do they do this? Do they do it because they've seen somebody else do it and it looks nice? Or does it help the players achieve a transferable skill set? In a classroom setting, a master teacher does things applicable to their students that will move them to the next level of learning. As a result, they can not only maximize their achievement on a test but also draw on that knowledge when some real-world application requires it.

I base every move I teach to players in my player development work on what I did as a player to achieve success. I explain the use of each move to them. For example, for the inside-foot advantage, I show them how running down the sideline and making sure your foot gets the advantage can give you the edge. Just like in life, when you get and use the advantage, you win. In basketball, having separation skills—the ability to get distance between you and the defender—allows you to get an advantage. And then when I go into all the little specifics of advantage, they go, "My God, he knows the finer details."

I was blessed to have great coaches along my path. And I think you will find in every walk of life that the people who have had success had someone who taught them the why along with the how—or someone who emulated those. Coach Fimbres had a simple approach and methodology. He was also encouraging. We didn't do a whole lot, but we didn't need to. He taught us we just needed to get a certain skill set to have success. His approach wasn't overly demanding; he based it on the idea that basketball is a simple game and if we became fundamentally strong, we could execute what we practiced daily.

At that time in my life, as a sixth, seventh, and eighth grader, I was just coming into my body, with all the growing pains of my body maturing. During those years, you're very awkward. You're like a baby horse, learning how to do things. So building confidence takes encouragement. At that level, a coach needs to be encouraging. Then you feel it's all right if you fail. You're just getting to the required skill set. And then in high school, I remained fortunate to have people who challenged our team appropriately for our level. At the varsity level in high school, people pay money to watch you play.

You face more pressure to play well and perform. Playing the game becomes more demanding. And you also have more things that demand your time and attention. For a whole lot of people, this represents the pinnacle of their basketball career.

People don't understand it when a player misses a key shot. It's difficult; you won't make them all. But the work that goes on behind the scenes separates people. That's why you have people like Kobe Bryant, who had unbelievable work ethic and drive, because they know success is all performance based. There's no substitution for it. Before becoming a college athlete, I was fortunate to be taken under the wing of a gentleman named Gerald Reece, who had led the country in scoring when he was a college player and was now going to become a professional athlete. I was a high school kid at the time and in awe of him as a player because he was so intense and wanted to be the best, to go hard, and to work hard. And when we met, I told him I was going to play basketball in college the next year, so we worked and worked and worked.

Every day posed a challenge. We worked on skill sets a lot, and then we played live one-on-one full court. We would play ten games like that. In basketball terminology, we call that *the truth*. In this format, you have no way to escape or hide. Either you get by the defender and score or you don't. And on the other side, you must defend him, or else he scores. It's the simple truth of basketball, as it reveals what you can and cannot do as a basketball player. It reveals your weaknesses not only physically but mentally, having to endure the test day in and day out with someone clearly better, stronger, and faster than you. I was determined to get better but felt out of place for a long time; I could shoot the ball and make baskets, but having to do that against someone who had completed his NCAA eligibility and finished as the leading scorer in the nation—well, that was another task.

Gerald trained religiously. And when we played full court, he never took it easy on me. He would go at a full sprint, running and dribbling the basketball down the court, dunking and shooting to try to beat me 10–0. To face someone that driven caused a shock to my system. We trained daily, and I observed his work ethic, his habits, and what he tried to teach me. He taught me how to play above the line—to play above what I was used to. He taught me to compete, to demand myself to improve, to not quit, and certainly to not blame anyone, complain, or defend my actions.

He always told me how he was going to attack me before he did. It was fantastic because each trip down the court provided me with an opportunity to learn about my opponent and what to give him and what to try to take away. I learned about speed. I learned about cutting the court in half and how I could give myself a better chance, especially with someone running full speed. The farther away from the basket, the better for me. I also learned that I had to use my footwork to get away from him, as he was strong and wanted to put his body and muscle against me to pressure me to turn the ball over.

Gerald would try to humiliate me. Many times, he did beat me 10–0, until I figured out not only how to handle the pressure but also how to get my shot off quickly. I eventually won some games, and when we concluded for the summer and it came time for me to go off to UC–Santa Cruz, I was so prepared that I could play in the starting lineup even as a college freshman. I brought a readyset-go mentality to work hard, develop my skills, and go full speed that worked so fast that the reality of a game seemed slow to me, and thus, I could see the game in a slow-motion-type way and score easier. This mentality worked. It shocked me how ready I was for college basketball. From that point on, after training with Gerald, I've always said the game is quite simple; you put the ball in the basket, and you stop the other team from doing the same. That's what it boils down to.

From that experience with Gerald, I was head and shoulders above my peers at college because they didn't understand that work ethic. They didn't know I did this nonstop, in the morning, in the afternoon, and at night. That's generally true of all the great basketball players. Nobody knows how much time they put in. They don't see all that. And by the time people do witness these players, they are amazed at these players' confidence. That confidence is born out of all that unseen practice and drive and makes it so that when they see their opponent, they know in their heart they will outwork and outplay their opponent, and they will win. They believe that person across from them hasn't done half the work they've done.

That's where their credibility comes from—not only their player statistics but the fact that they can demonstrate how and why they got where they are. It comes from putting in all those hours. I provide my players with the same type of work and rigorous learning that I did as a player because it provides them with a sense of where they are and where they need to be. Once they've developed the confidence and credibility that come with this learning, they can feel a difference when they are in a game; they can listen more attentively, as they have paid attention to details all along and can now demonstrate those skills in a game.

Anytime a coach goes into a new environment, it causes a cultural shift. *Culture* refers to how the coach and team will do things. What is their

You Can't Make the Shot
If You Never Take It

When I was a college basketball player at UC–San Diego, our team hosted our own basketball tournament during winter break. One of the things our coach had taught us was to cut the court in half when we played defense. For me, as a point guard, that meant keeping my opponent from crossing over to the other half of the court. And when a player went below the free-throw line, we never let him back out of the box. So with that philosophy in mind, we reached the championship game and were playing a team from Massachusetts. They were nationally ranked, so it was a big deal. Simply put, we wanted to do everything that we could to win the game on our home court.

They had an excellent point guard, whom I was called on to stick with and defend all night. Keep in mind I was not a defensive specialist. I was an offensive scoring guy. The loneliest place on earth is playing defense on somebody one-on-one. But because of the system that we learned, on defense, we would force a player to our help or to the sideline or the baseline. If that player touched any part of the sideline, it was like having a sixth man. That caused a turnover, and it became our ball. The same was true if the player touched any part of the baseline. It was like having a seventh man on defense. We used to practice how to get three stops in a row to see if collectively, as a team, we could communicate and stop the ball. This toughened us up mentally.

I remember coming out of time-outs as we needed to get two critical stops in the game and knowing I would be on an island when that point guard came up the court. If I didn't get the ball out of his hands, out of the middle of the floor, then I had to decide whether I would stay with the player or force him to my help. It's reassuring in a team sport to hear your teammates tell you, "I've got your help on the right" or "I've got you on the left." This support gives you added incentive to play better. It gives you bravado. It makes you stronger. You are more willing to take up the challenge.

As it got near two minutes left in the game, we needed to get a stop every time. In the last two minutes of a close game, it's about executing, getting to the free-throw line, and imposing your will on the other team's will. That was my responsibility: to force this point guard somewhere other than where he wanted to go. Now, most teams begin with some sort of set play, usually to the right side of the floor because most players are right-hand dominant. So the defensive call was to cut the court in half and force the ball to the left side of the floor. I had to decide to pick up the player at either full court or half court and see what I could do to impose my will. As that went on, I decided to lunge at the ball every once in a while to see if I could get a crucial turnover without ever having to reach or block a shot. So I tried to see if I could confuse the player.

Keep in mind the whole time, I was trying to get him to go to the left side of the floor, which is a guarded position because most players are very tentative to come up with the left hand. During the three or four trips down the floor, he knew I was guiding him down the left side, and he got acclimated to it. Those last thirty seconds of the game included tense moments. Finally, I decided I would stunt again. I would take a risk. So I lunged violently to the left in a fake opportunity so the player would automatically shift to his dominant right hand, and when he did, I was there. I put my hand on the ball, got the steal, and went for a layup. After that, his team had to call a time-out to stop our momentum.

I remember sitting down on the bench, thinking, *My God, that stunt worked!* I was able to take a chance on something I had not done before and ended up scoring a crucial basket as a result, allowing us to come away with the victory.

A number of players come from a background that considers missing a shot or taking a risk on defense a bad thing, and they get yelled at for it. I have that in my background as well. I had a coach in one of my earlier years who was very demanding. Others even viewed him as demeaning, because every time any of us missed a shot, he made it a really big deal. But I do have to say, though I don't agree with that technique, the pressure of his yelling really did help me later on because I became proficient at what I did to avoid his yelling. But the key is not yelling or fretting over missed shots; it is doing the work and practicing it. Confidence comes from continuous repetition. You have to be careful, though, because you can repeat mistakes. You can take a thousand shots with wrong form, and the ball won't go in. You have to repeat things properly.

I have had a lot of players who have been coached to fear. *If I take the shot, boy, this has to go in,* they think. Even to this day, I assure my higher-level teams that they are in a different environment now. We have to build absolute confidence, not have players wonder and question themselves when they have a chance to shoot. When I work on shooting with my teams, a lot of the work involves situational practice, with time and score limits, distractions, and especially pressure. My philosophy is that pressure is a privilege. Not a lot of people in the world get to go into an arena and face a pressure situation that causes butterflies in their stomach. My job is to get a player to move away from fear of taking a shot when it matters most so they have confidence to succeed in such an environment.

I play golf periodically, and I see guys lose it on the golf course—throwing their clubs, yelling at the ball, arms in the air. I remember one golf coach who asked me a key question one day when I was playing with him. He asked, "How many hours a day do you practice golf?" I replied that I had only played that week and maybe a few times all year. He simply noted that I shouldn't worry about how I played that day since it wasn't like I put a lot of time into it; he told me to just enjoy the atmosphere, the outdoors, and the camaraderie.

I contrasted that lack of work with my effort in my collegiate basketball skills. I had definitely put in the work there. And out of that time and effort I had put in to get better came this sense of accomplishment, pride, and worthiness that made me think I deserved to take the shot. I sensed that my repetition exceeded everybody else's. So I felt I had every right to take the shot and, more likely than not, it would go in the basket.

I remember driving down the freeway in LA and passing USC at eight in the morning. As I looked over at the campus, I thought about how many hours of work I had already done that morning while the sun was barely coming up on campus. I had finished my workout before many at this institution woke up. When I would play, I was ready to take the shot because I knew I had done it thousands of times before. But my workout was different from just shooting a ball. I changed it up and used the term from Coach Whitsitt, who called it a *discipline* because I needed to discipline my mind and body to make shots without hitting the rim. I trained to not hit the rim at all, and if I did, I would start all over again with whatever set amount of shots that I had determined for that morning. The goal was to not hit the rim at all. That led me to the scientific part of shooting: thinking about the ball's trajectory, paying attention to how to lift that trajectory, and considering where the shot came from. I ran through a checklist and asked myself, *Does it come from my legs, my elbow, or my wrist? How do I get quicker so I can get that shot off instantly?* That's the transformation caused by repetition, and that's what makes players like Stephen Curry so unique; the amount of work that he does before a game far exceeds what most people do in their practices. Some athletes take the power of repetition for granted. The great ones work with discipline.

In practice, I emphasize the act of taking the key shot. I never want a player to worry about taking the shot. Worrying is a destructive habit. There's always the next play. That's the beauty of basketball. You always have something else to do, and you have to do it immediately. So when you do get another shot, the players often have to self-correct because the coach can't always call a time-out to fix up a play. You have to self-correct based on repetition. That's why most players develop a routine for things they have to do over and over again. You see this especially at the free-throw line because at that line, a player is all alone and repeatedly shoots from the same place. The really good players can close their eyes for this because they have developed a muscle-memory reflex from shooting this shot over and over again. They also can exercise the power of visualization without even having the basketball; when their mind does this out of habit, the body naturally follows. That's been proven in Olympic sports; Olympians will do an act over and over again in their mind. Without having to overtrain, they visualize their event as if they already swam or ran the race. And sometimes, because they've done it so much in their mind, their body simply falls in line and makes it a reality.

Visualize the success you wish to have in whatever endeavor you try. What does your business meeting look like in your mind? What does closing your deal look like? You can see it in your mind first, and then, you can act it out enough over and over until it becomes second nature. I believe the best sales teams constantly practice, even in their heads, and visualize success.

Slumps prove how much success comes from the mind leading the body. Slumps can happen to anybody in sports and in business. To get myself out of a basketball slump once, I had to reach two realizations to get there.

1. I had to know that I chose to be great or extraordinary at something.
2. I had to know what it took to achieve this greatness: creating the process and mastering the details.

Once I had reached these two realizations, then I was ready to take risks because I had prepared myself for these risks. In a sense, with these realizations, risks are no longer risks, per se, but calculated efforts toward success. To illustrate, when the father of Laird Hamilton, the big-wave surfer, asked his son, "Laird, why do you take all these risks with your life, surfing these humongous waves?" Laird said, "Dad, I've been preparing all my life to be surfing those waves." Risk taking is as essential in sports as it is in life.

When I was a senior at UCSD, trying to fit in, I made everyone around me better and didn't shoot the ball as much as I used to. I remember one of my coaches at UCSD, Coach Aumann, taking me aside and trying to discover, along with the other coaches, how he could help me out of my slump. Coach Aumann suggested that I go back to the place where I first fell in love with the game. I took that advice and returned to Tucson during one of our breaks. There in Tucson, I walked down the street from my house where I grew up to C.E. Rose School, where I fell in love with the game. The moment I started walking down the street, I felt different because the joy was coming back. The smell of the surrounding grass; the sensation of the sharp, crisp air; and all my old feelings came rushing back. Those familiar feelings start to give you that extra energy you need. Much of a slump is mental, and sometimes, it is caused by overtraining, and your body is just tired. After I took that mental journey, I returned fresh and happy. Now, I could concentrate on the details and the feeling of having the ball go through the net.

When you find yourself in a slump, you can overthink the game, something both coaches and players do. I don't make slumping players overanalyze what they are doing. I ask them to describe in detail to me where and when they first fell in love with the game. Usually, right then, you get this happiness that comes out of them—this joy. From that joy, we can then go back to work. Another thing that I do is score their work with music, like a movie score. The old black-and-white movies are great in a way, but they lack color. Then there are quiet movies that you really have to pay attention to. But when you add color and music to movies, that's when you have drama, flair, and intensity. I do that to my workouts. Music adds intensity and scores the work the players put in. They grow more passionate because the music inspires them; it gets them into the work. Before I know it, they are working harder than when I just used my voice to tell them what to do. Then the energy and creativity come rushing in, and the practice goes to a whole different level.

All walks of life can get mundane. In a business environment, it might not be possible to use music like that, but it is possible to find creative ways to get people to enjoy the day-to-day process. I try to inspire others on my team, as a business manager or owner does. A guy by the name of WRDSMTH writes simply tremendous tags all over the city of Los Angeles, and one of his tags especially stands out to me: "Aspire to inspire others and the universe will take notice." That's exactly what I want to do: inspire somebody to get outside a comfort zone and to think outside the proverbial box. I want people to consider what it's like to hear the word *yes* when they say they want to try new things, instead of always hearing the word *no*.

You only get one goaround in life, and opportunities to do great or new things don't come around that often. I get to live one time, and I want it to be the best experience I can possibly have. What does that entail? A lot of people think that it entails growing up in a certain area and staying there for forty years. But those people never get to see anything else, to experience anything else. For some people, that might be great, but I want more. I want to be able to take a walk with my family later in life and relive our good memories—not talk about the dreams we never went after and the things we didn't do. I go wherever life takes me because I see each new turn as an opportunity even when I don't know where it will lead me. You never know unless you take a chance. You can always come back home, but you can't always leave.

Life throws a lot of obstacles at you. You have to be willing to fight through them and take risks. As I have, you must keep driving through tough times to prevent yourself from having regrets. But to achieve that, you need to have a laserlike focus on your goal, or your shot. To have success in any endeavor, you have to work hard. You have to want to compete. No one can give this desire to you. You have to go get it.

If you have properly prepared for the key moment, a risk for most people won't be a risk for you. Great players have a system, and this system includes repetition and preparation for the moment. Taking risks is key to any success. Don't be afraid to take the shot.

Enjoy the Journey

In my rookie season as a professional basketball player, 1985–1986, I am coming off of leading the United States in scoring among Divisions I, II, and III. We're playing against another league team, and it's a time-out situation as the other team is about to shoot a free throw. The game is on the line. The other team has a one-and-one opportunity, which means if the player shooting free throws makes the first free throw, he'll get another one. Once he takes his shot or shots, we have to get down the court with three seconds left in the game. With three seconds, you essentially have time for one dribble or one long pass, and then, the shot has to go up. If their player makes one free throw, they go up one; if he makes both, they're up two.

During the time-out, our coach designs a play, saying, "So here we are at the free-throw line. We're going to have mass confusion at the line, and we're going to talk and talk and talk as if we're trying to organize ourselves, essentially to provide a distraction, without getting a technical foul for distracting. We're going to look at each other." Essentially, I have our best rebounder on my right side, so whether the guy at the line makes it or misses it, we're ready. If their player makes it, our guy has to immediately get out-of-bounds and inbound the ball to me, and I'll have one dribble, and I'll take the shot. However, if he misses the shot, then our player can kick that rebound out long to me, without any thought.

We have a decoy, though, because we have another player next to our best rebounder saying loudly that he'll be right there to get the pass as soon as our guy rebounds the ball or inbounds it. This way, the other team's players think they kind of know where the ball will go. The real play called is that if the free throw is missed, then our best rebounder will get the rebound and kick it to me, and I will cross half court and rise up and shoot the ball.

During the time-out, as part of the decoy, we start acting like we've got all this confusion and ask for the ball on the other side of the court. After we finally line up for the free throws, the first one is good. But the whole time, our two guys are talking: "If he makes this free throw, you get me the ball." The coaches add to this from the sidelines. They're saying, "Get the ball to the other side … the other side."

The free-throw shooter misses the second shot. My rebounder grabs it and in midair turns and kicks it right to me at the half-court mark. I take one good long dribble, which leads me to almost the three-point line. There, I rise up, I have an excellent look at the basket, I let the shot fly, and the ball goes in. It is pandemonium.

Despite what most fans think when they watch sports, it's not really the end of the game that most athletes remember, or even the victory or loss. I think when you talk to most people who have been through events like that, not the outcome but the entire journey matters most to them. For every championship that I've won, either as a player or as a coach, the friendships I've developed and the road trips and the experiences I've had along the way have mattered more to me. I inevitably ask all my players later in their lives what the score was of this or that game that was important or memorable to them. They don't know. They don't remember it. But they all can describe in detail everything that happened the day of that game, from when they arrived at the hotel the night before, to when they woke up on game day, to where they went after that, to what it felt like showing up at the arena. They know all those details, all those experiences that led up to the final score. And in totality, over an entire season, the conditioning phase, the preparation they went through to get them ready to win a championship—that's what the majority of them remember. That's what remains the most magnified in their head. Take the movie *Rocky*. What moves everybody who watches this movie is the preparation and struggle that Rocky goes through. It's the journey leading to that final moment.

Once you have won, it feels wonderful; however, what comes next? "One Shining Moment" is such a popular montage of the NCAA tournament because the final night is climactic. The tournament itself, the drama of it highlighted in the montage, is what is so exciting and what people cannot get enough of. They enjoy all the stories of the Davids slaying the giants, of the hero making the shot at the buzzer, of the tense moments at the end of the game. Those things that lead up to the final game and final buzzer are memorable.

I can truly remember all the processes I went through as a player—all the practices, failures, and ups and downs. I know that things paid off and all those little details ended up being big in the end. And I remember how thankful I was to have that push to develop my skill set to allow me to have success shooting the ball and running a team. It took our coach's wisdom for me to see that if my teammates and I all surrendered to our team's set process and trusted each other, we would get somewhere and achieve something, together.

Championship rings are not the most important thing. Who we became along the way is most important. To this day, my former players come see my current players, and they see their younger selves in them. Politeness and manners count—my players look people in the eye, shake hands firmly. My former players see that in current players, and they remember they did that once upon a time. And those little gestures go a long way. They send a message. They separate us from other teams and other players. I think this process I use is unique; I drill it into players before they even pick up a basketball or learn a specific skill set.

I want the experience of basketball under my supervision to be more than just winning or losing a game. I consider the purpose of my relationship with players to enhance the spirit of life. That's what I want to do. I want to enhance the experience we have together. Later, I want my players to fondly remember what it was like to play for me and how all the hard work paid off, win or lose.

You hear people say a game trip is a business trip. That mind-set focuses on winning and losing. Really, you don't have to eliminate the joy that the trip or work can bring. For example, my OC Magic AAU team took a trip to Las Vegas so they could play in a national tournament. We made the journey about more than the games and the tournament, though. It was meant to be educational and fun; we made sure while we were there, they could see something that would take their breath away. We drove straight to the Hoover Dam, and I allowed one of my coaches to get as much information as he could so that he could in essence be the tour guide and help the players understand this awe-inspiring architectural marvel. Then we got to the hotel and had team bonding, room assignments, duties, and responsibilities for each room. All this happened the day and night before the games even started. When the players went to their Saturday morning game, they competed, played with a spirit of fun, and gave of themselves and for their teammates because they shared a bond around common experiences. They will remember these outside-the-game experiences more than any game they played that weekend.

I want players to ask, "Why is basketball so fun?" They can also learn a lot from the sport, for sure, like how to deal with pressure, but I want to make sure they have fun. As a head coach, when two teams enter a building, I can clearly tell which one has a better chance of winning the game, regardless of their talent, by how they walk in. You can see when a team is bonding. They smile, they have fun, and they give one another high fives. And when you take that same chemistry onto the court, magic occurs. It's unbelievable what can happen. All the best teams have that chemistry.

In the era when Pete Carroll was head football coach at USC, the Trojans created something remarkable. Carroll always had these intense practices, but these practices also had a sense of fun, excitement, and joy. The result was hard to beat—literally. That team had an undeniable chemistry that showed off the field and proved itself on the field as well over several years. Carroll worked hard to make his team's experiences unique and fun, and as a result, they were willing to go through the proverbial wall for him and each other.

Some coaches forget to build experiences for teams to enjoy each other as part of their process. They make their time together just about basketball, and they make it hard, and then, some players quit. There's much more to having success than that. You can get much more out of people if you think empathetically. How my players feel when they go into the arena gives me the edge. I know if my players feel good, we have a solid chance of winning. Even if the two teams' talent isn't evenly matched, I can tell when we have better energy. We have better chemistry. So our player will dive onto the floor for a loose ball when the other team's player won't do that. And that one possession could make the difference.

My professional coaching experience has been laced with others' undervaluation of chemistry. I think in other countries particularly, general managers and owners believe that if you pay this player a certain salary, that player will have twenty-five points a game. That is true to a degree. That is that player's typical performance. But how you get that performance to mix with everyone else's makes the difference. Players are not robots. They are human beings who need inspiration. Each game, they will go through a shootaround when they get into the arena. But what emotion will come with it on a given day?

When you play a team that has chemistry and they're loose, and they laugh and smile and share a special bond, you will have a very difficult time beating that team. When you look at the history of all sports, you'll see chemistry has been the deciding factor for every team that has won an NFL Super Bowl, an NBA Finals, an MLB World Series, an NHL Stanley Cup Finals—what have you. Each of these teams had a unique quality that other teams didn't have.

Conversely, one bad seed on a good team can ruin everything. I know from experience on my pro teams, where hiring players is usually out of my control, sometimes you will indeed get a bad person in terms of chemistry. And it sucks the life out of everything. Playing becomes nothing more than a job. You'll see the team come into the building with frowns. They'll do the work because they want to still get paid, but playing doesn't have joyful emotions attached to it. After the game, they'll leave, and that's that.

This has happened to me several times on my professional teams. Each team goes through a number of transformations in the course of a season, with injuries or a lack of player performance, which can result in players getting fired and new ones being brought in. Many owners and general managers will look at a player coming in as a way to help the team win instantly, but a player change usually comes with a price. When a player change occurs during the season, that player comes in with an expectation and also a disadvantage. The expectation is to produce. The disadvantage comes from his not having time to build relationships with his new teammates or coaching staff.

Players I didn't agree with have been selected for my team; I disagreed with their selection not in terms of their playing skills but in terms of baggage that they would bring to the team. This lack of chemistry caused us to have to reevaluate our situation and think immediately of solutions to make our process guide us to victories. Many times, as head coach, I have felt powerless, as I have known that this one poor selection would drain the entire team of everything positive that we had built up. It takes only one bad selection to realize this. And when you are a head coach overseas, you are expected to develop a team in no time. All owners, general managers, and fans want to win the championship that night—no excuses.

Many teams have 10-80-10 percentages. This means 10 percent of a team are the overachievers, the ones putting in the extra work on their craft before and after practice. Then the middle 80 percent of the team do what is expected but not much more before or after practice. Then the bottom 10 percent drain the team's energy; they don't give all they have in terms of their work ethic not only in their skill development but also in their team chemistry. These players need to be cut and released before they poison the others.

I gauge my success by what my players do before practice and after practice. I watch how they come into the building. If they come into the building walking kind of fast—walking with purpose—then they're happy; they've arrived. If after practice, I see they're still hanging around, laughing, and sharing with each other, then we've been successful. It's the process that brings that happiness. The wins will come because of all the other positive things that happen throughout the day.

The top coaches try to concentrate on staying upbeat, focused, motivated, and positive. They are demanding yet enthusiastic and encouraging. Players know if you are a fake and phony coach. They know if you present who you truly are. There's nothing like walking the walk. Many coaches, business owners, and CEOs say, "Do as I say," but they don't do it themselves. They don't put themselves in that vulnerable position. Having vulnerability lets your team and your employees know you are in this together. You all share in the enjoyable moments and the work. Maybe you will win the games, but as time goes on and you reflect back on your work, you won't remember the opponents; you'll remember the experiences and the times you had together. When people go through good experiences together, it brings them together.

Interestingly, many coaches remember the losses more than they remember the wins. That's because rigorous preparation goes into setting up for a win, and when they lose, they feel determined to learn from the loss. *Why did we not win? What happened?* They ponder. And they focus on what they could have done better. Coaches are, at heart, troubleshooters. They seek to fix problems. That's what makes losing a learning process. After a loss, good coaches ask themselves critical questions. For example, if you ask yourself, *Why can't I make a basket?* Your brain will give you fifty reasons why you can't make one. It's because you don't get enough sleep, you don't eat right, you're slow, and you don't get to the gym on time, and so on. But if you ask yourself, *What can I do to make this shot?* You will come up with answers that can solve the problem. *I can change the trajectory on the ball. I can be quicker. Am I on my toes? Is my elbow above my eyebrow?* Your mind will now find solutions. Good coaches answer critical questions so they can fix problems that cause losses.

I ask my players, "If I left you inside the gym and turned off all the lights, what would you do? Would you just sit there? Would you check for unlocked doors or push on a door? Would you get frustrated and eventually try to break the doors down?" The point of my asking these questions is to encourage them to determine a way out with proactive, positive thinking. The mind starts seeking solutions, like pushing on every door or checking the windows, but only because you asked a better critical question. That's what I want all my guys to do: ask better questions. That's true in business too. You might ask yourself, *Why am I not getting those calls?* And you'll come up with all the reasons why not. But try changing your approach to framing questions. Ask yourself instead, *What can I do to get the sale?* Now, your mind will find solutions. You'll attack the issue from a different, useful angle.

This happens with most good coaches when we lose games. We ask ourselves the basic question, *Why did we lose?* And we might answer, *Maybe we didn't prepare well enough.* And other actionable thoughts like that will present themselves. Some coaches don't ask themselves better questions. They just maintain a woe-is-me feeling. That's what makes them miserable. But when they get to asking themselves great questions like *What can we do to get better?* it empowers them. It makes them think, *We can do this.* Now, they feel driven. They don't focus on the loss anymore; they focus on the solution and move forward on their journey, toward winning.

People tend to think success in sports is all about physical talent. But the differentiator is your mentality. Success has to start in your mind, and I am proof of that. When I get excited, it starts out in the head first, and then comes the enthusiasm. It makes my work more energetic. But if you have a negative attitude when you walk into the gym, things will not get any better. That's when some coaches yell and scream. Their success won't get any better.

I want to underscore and repeat the value of the journey. In a sense, the journey never ends, nor the important aspects of it that you can actually *share* with others later. Most players and coaches can't recall the scores of the wins or losses later in life. But they can share aspects of the journey; most of the time, they are vivid memories and provide that happiness and sense of accomplishment when relived in their minds. This is not a small detail.

Getting to that one shining moment takes a long process—a process that is far more important and far more memorable than the final outcome. But it all starts in the head and the heart. The physical will come; so will the result, win or lose, but the journey is the key—not one moment in time. Enjoy as many of these times as you can.

You Can't Control Everything

I remember a time in college at UC–San Diego when I had to trust my teammate to make a last-second shot. We had three excellent scorers on our team, and one of us was usually called on at various crucial times to make a last shot. We had a lot of misdirection plays where I would get the ball, go off to the other side of the court, and then find the player I needed to find. This particular time, the play had me pass the ball to the right side of the court and go get the ball back, and then, that player would take off under the rim and come off a single or double screen on the other side. I was used to seeing that play. We had run it over and over. We just had different adjustments that went on from it.

To get that play to work, you have to sell that you will be the person with the ball; that is the key. The person with the ball is the most important person on the court. When you can make everyone believe you are a threat when you have the ball—that you are the person who's going to score—all eyes stay on you. Sometimes, the defenders converge. Sometimes, they overcompensate.

And that's what happened here, because I could see the defenders saw when I turned the corner coming off my own screen, which provided some drama since I was getting into the heart of the defense. And they had to freeze a little bit, allowing me to get into the lane. While I looked for my shot, I had to set up my player. I knew how he liked to come off his screen—how he liked to flare on the baseline side. As I distracted the defense, I just needed to pass the ball crisply with my left hand to his right ear so he could catch it in motion. I thought the play went great. The outcome was our player was hot, he put up a great shot, and of course, he made it.

We all have wants in life. For example, I want to provide for my family. I want stability. There's also what you have. I have a great wife. I have great sons. I have the love of my players and the support of my family and friends. I have a sense of humor. Part of the definition of *wanting* is that it's the opposite of *having*. But the thing is if you want anything, you have to let go of wanting it.

Ask yourself, *Can I let go of wanting to figure things out?* That's part of what I talk to athletes about. I tell them they should ask themselves, *Can I let go of wanting to know what to do? Can I let go of wanting to know the answers? Even disapproval of myself—can I let go of that? Can I give myself approval?* That's the ticket to success. You need a lot of things in life that require you to surrender control.

We all seek approval; we seek control; we seek security. How do you get out of wanting those things? It can require digging deeper. Ask yourself, *Whom or what do I judge? Whom or what do I reject? Whom or what do I resist? What am I jealous of? Can I let all of that go?* We all feel the need to hold on to things. When I look at such an attachment, I ask myself, *What's the advantage of holding on to this?* And then, I imagine holding on to it no longer. *What's the advantage or disadvantage of me holding on to it?* I ponder. You can apply this thinking to every part of your life.

Now, there is another side to holding on to things. *What do I like about holding on? What don't I like about it?* These are questions that I ask internally on a daily basis; I try to explain them to my coaches and my athletes. "What's the advantage of letting go of this thing you are holding on to?" I ask them. I want them to know it's okay to surrender control. It's all right to say, "I don't know the answer." It's all right to allow yourself not to be liked. We hold on to so many things that we're not really sure about. Trust probably plays a big part in that. What's the advantage of having trust? What's the disadvantage? Again, I say, "Imagine never being able to trust ever again. How does that make you feel?" These are deep, personal things. Could you let go of your entire attachment to trusting?

Once you get to that place where you decide you can let go of your attachments, you have to ask yourself how you will let go of them. That's the needed technique. You have to want to be calm. You have to want self-assurance more than you want control, more than you want approval, and more than you want security. I find it really helps to wake up in the morning aware of what you are feeling and trace those feelings down to the underlying wants. I ask myself, *Why do I feel the way I do? Is it because I want control? Is it because I want approval? Or is it because I want security?* And then, I see if I can surrender throughout the day and let those feelings go, over and over. This holds especially true when I feel stressed. I can notice the feeling and say, *Oh man, I feel like this because I want control of this situation. I have to recognize I have no control over this situation, so I might as well let this thing go the way it is.* Basically, I'll just surrender to the circumstance, the people, and the resistance. When I do that, good feelings come up. Generally, the feelings are rooted in the now—like *right now, I have to do something.* That's pretty much all I can ask for; right now is the key to surrendering.

Anything I say to my athletes I have already done myself. All the things that I teach, I did them already. I learned how to do inside-foot advantage, step-backs. I did them over and over again. When the Chicago Bulls invited me to be a free agent, I was the last guy cut, but I went in there understanding that I was going to give my all and leave with no regrets. I went in there with no expectation that I would make it, just that I would work hard daily. Every time I got the ball, I told my teammates I was not going to dribble in the backcourt. I surrendered control of the team. Every time I got the ball, I told them I would pass ahead and they were to go ahead and look to create and score. If they gave the ball back to me, then I would go ahead and shoot and score. As a result, I never turned the ball over. I never got embarrassed in the backcourt, and I ended up scoring a lot of points because I gave my teammates the ball. In surrendering control of the team, inevitably, I gained complete control of the team because they understood I made sacrifices for them. I surrendered my scoring for their happiness. Concentrating only on what was in front of me made me happy.

Each day, I asked myself one question: *What do I have to do today so I don't get sent home?* And every day I practiced, I asked myself a simple question: *What can I do today a little bit better than the last time I practiced?* A lot of times, I felt super frustrated. But that was my learning curve at a young age as I continuously looked for self-improvement. People don't want to give up control when they have a car, a mortgage, and a job to worry about. I think that's why people sometimes lose their minds; they try to control a situation when they can't, rather than saying, "You know what, it's out of my control. We're just going to have fun right now, and we'll figure this out." That's why I always say to my team and coaches, "There's always a solution; let's figure out what that solution is." Sometimes, we aren't in the right frame of mind to find a solution because we want approval. We want to feel significant. We all want to feel others approve of what we do.

But what do we do if it doesn't get approval? Do we hold on to something that will lead us down a path to internal destruction? You bet most of us do that. I have some special processes that I use to avoid this bad path. One is I focus on the face of the person who has done something wrong to me. And I ask myself these questions one at a time: *Do I want control? Am I looking for approval? What am I seeking here—security?* I keep doing this internal review so I can let that person be him- or herself. I do this in situations where maybe somebody frustrates me and I have to look at him or her and look at myself and ask, *Is this person trying to control me? Am I trying to control this person?* Usually, I realize this wrong against me isn't anything other than my needing to let go of my sense of control and wanting that person to be someone else. Most of the time, there isn't any real problem.

Most of the time, my players think they just want success. And if you ask a young coach what he wants, he might say he just wants to make a lot of money. It's like people think money solves all problems and is the key to a successful life. But money doesn't buy character or give you charisma or class. I ask my players what they would do if they had all the abundance in the world. Where would they go? How would they act? What would they buy? When you ask that, you find out what they really want; they want approval, they want control, or they want safety. By asking that, I can find out right then and there where we stand.

Somewhere in there, you start to discover that all these wants really come down to the three main wants: (1) certainty and comfort, (2) uncertainty and variety, and (3) significance. You don't really need these things. Needs and wants are two different things. And then, you get to another place, and you realize what you already have meets the needs that matter most. I, for example, have the love of my wife. I have the love of my sons. I have seen the world. I have learned to talk to all kinds of people from all over the world in my life.

I teach the concept of understanding wants to others, to my family, and to my players, especially, by spending time with them. I can walk into the room and talk to them, but it doesn't give the same impression as spending real time with them. When you give of your time, it demonstrates to others that they can feel comfortable, share with you, and have an understanding that they are important. When you are able to share with others about life's ups and downs and experiences that you have had by being an open book, that is appreciated by so many because you are being vulnerable. I've had a ton of failures. I don't believe people when they say they've never made a mistake or when they judge you as if they have never made a mistake. They have. They just don't want you to know it. But the moment you know, your conversation comes from a different place. Experience comes from failure, and the greatest life lessons have come from that. When I teach that to my sons or to my players, I take myself off a pedestal. I think people appreciate it when you are open and honest and real, including about your mistakes. People also appreciate it when you give them your undivided time and attention.

I appreciate Coach Wooden so much because he taught me about the value of undivided attention. One day when I was visiting him, his house phone rang and rang. It absolutely stunned me how many calls came in and how he completely ignored them. He did not interrupt our conversation to pick up his phone and treat that person as more important than me—at least not at that moment. His time was with me and not on that phone. I even stopped our conversation at one point to say, "Coach, don't you want to get that?" He answered, "No, I'm with you. I will get back to them later." I walked away in awe of that and never forgot it. And subsequent to that, when I would call him and I'd get his answering machine, I understood that it meant he was with someone else, and that's how it went. He'd get back to you when he got back to you. Whoever was with him was most important at that moment. So I try to give my attention wholeheartedly.

When you look at people and you look at your past, often, the success of your relationships and work comes down to quality of time spent. When my players want to make every shot or they are not willing to do the extra work, they're indicating to me that they're trying to stay in control. For example, on the defensive side, I want my players to take the chance to go for the ball when another player is trying to influence the ball toward his help. For that to happen, they have to surrender control. They have to believe when they do that, they won't look bad. That's why I tell them they have to surrender; they have to stop thinking they are in high school. I say that because too often in high school, players get yelled at and don't want to risk that or being sat down for a mistake. I want players to learn to trust the guy next to them on their team. I want them to let go and go for it. I say, "Your teammate will cover for you if you don't get the ball. And if they score on us, so what? It's two points. On to the next play. I want us to feel this way all the time. I'm going to trust you. You're going to trust me. We're going to work together." That creates harmony, unity, and a bond because all the team members can say they're not looking for control; they're not necessarily seeking approval; and that want for security—well, they have security because they trust one another. Our teams really look good when they play with that unity. With that harmony, if we lose a game, it's because the other team was better. It wasn't because of any other thing. And that's how it should be. You can leave the gym happy, not down and disappointed.

So many coaches in the world think the stuff of success happens on its own. They think you can walk into a building, and boom, you get hired. Putting on a uniform, playing in a beautiful building—none of that stuff matters. People matter. This exact thing happens in business. In business, most people start out with career and financial goals, and an attachment to money persists. If you work in business, you need to think about what your goals are and ask the question, *What advantage does having money give me?* Well, with money, you can pay off bills, purchase things without hesitation, and have security. Now, you start to see the reason for the attachment to money—the advantages of it.

But what are the disadvantages of having money? You have to pay taxes. Money may make you distrustful of people with less money. You think you must have a bigger house. So in business, you also have to ask this question: Imagine never having money again. Could you let go of your attachment to it? Part of the question for a businessperson is this: What do you like about money, and what don't you like about it? Inevitably, that leads to the next question or concern of approval—approval of who you are. That will lead you to ask yourself why you disapprove of yourself. Can you let go of that disapproval of yourself?

Most will say they hate feeling defeated. So from there, you must progress to the next step, which is figuring things out. What's the advantage of figuring things out? You can say you did it on your own. You can say, "I have the solution." What's the disadvantage of figuring things out or getting to that level of the process? The pressure rests squarely on you. You are the one who has to come up with solutions. And sometimes, you then get to the place where you must have the courage to let go of always knowing the answer. And that's great. That sometimes comes with relief. And in that place, I am forced to come up with a better question to solve the next problem.

You have to surrender wanting control, approval, and security. And then, you will have those things. Things will just come. I am sure pride gets in the way for most of us. If you ask people what they feel proud of, what they approve of, what or who they reject, and who they think they are better than, and they manage to let go of those thoughts and attachments, the letting go can lead to a complete mental shift in those employees, players, or people. But all of it comes down to digging deeply and getting to the root of what really drives you and then having a willingness to let it all go. In doing so, the right things—the things you want and need—will find their way to you.

You must consider so many things in order to be happy. But mainly, you must let stuff go. If I don't do that, then I will hold on to stuff that burdens me—blocks me. The truth is I can't control anybody. The only person in the world I can control is me.

You Always Have a Choice

I realized that I was good at putting the ball in the basket. I already enjoyed the game, but I knew I could have something special when I was MVP of the CYO league in the eighth grade. After having attended my first basketball camp to become good at my skills, and winning the basketball championship with my St. John's team, I had my first chance at the all-star game at the end of our season. I wanted to show everyone that I was the best.

As we played the game, the East and West teams seemed evenly matched, and the game was close. I got fouled late in the fourth quarter and had to step up to the line to make two free throws in a high-pressure situation in the closing seconds. I remember Coach Jay John trying to give me instructions yet not distract me from what I had to do. I didn't approach the free-throw line until I got the instruction from him. He said if I made these two shots, then I had to get up and pressure the ball but not foul so that time would run out and we would win. I said to him, "You mean, after I make these two shots, to get up and pressure?" He looked at Coach Fimbres, they shook their heads, and he continued to tell me yes. Nodding and staring at Coach Fimbres, I made both free throws, we won the game, and I was named MVP.

At that moment, I knew I wanted to keep playing this game for as long as I could. Each level had a change in expectations. As I entered high school, I worked my way up to the opportunity to get invited to Five-Star Basketball Camp, where I learned to appreciate that I could play against the best in the country and return back to Tucson, inspired to get better. Having older players who played in the NCAA take an interest in me and tell me I was good enough to play at the next level inspired me and made me work harder. Playing outdoors at Oury Park made me realize the game was so pure, outside in the elements, with great players, trash-talking, and hard fouls. I loved every minute of this as I was challenged to perform and experiment as a scorer.

I have based my whole life on going after basketball and adjusting as I get closer to what I have tried to pursue overall in my life. Everybody's got a dream. When I sit down in an auditorium of college students, I know they were told to chase their dreams when they all were young. They gained all this confidence, energy, support, and love, and then, the dream killers come, and all of a sudden, they're in college, where they must be realistic and are constantly asked, "What are you going to do with that degree?" They hear, "Do you know how many people out there are trying to become actors and are starving?"

You hear all the negativity now. I'm not suggesting you quit—I say don't ever give in. Don't ever lose that passion. You pursue your acting passion, or whatever passion you have. You may have to modify and adjust it, but that's okay. You adapt so that you can stay in that passion and keep finding ways to pursue it.

I started in basketball, and I am still in it to this day. I am a prime example of doing whatever it takes to stay involved with your passion. But I had some moments when I got offtrack. I did what I thought I was supposed to do to bring home a check. But *I wasn't happy*. I realized I was pursuing money because I believed I had to. It's like when I was in college, I had no one to pave the way for me who said, "Choose a major you love." On the contrary, I heard, "You're going to go to college, and you need to major in something that will make you money."

So I majored in economics, of all things, which consists of calculus and graphs. Knowing what I know now, I would have chosen history or biology or something where I could have really enjoyed my pathway, because my major didn't matter anyway. My career path ended up being based on my passion. And I learned the truth of the saying that the average person changes careers five times. When you're younger, you don't believe it, but now, I know for sure it happens. Lots of pathways change.

I didn't know what I was supposed to do. That's why I went into making money. I went to law school, even knowing it was horrible for me and I was just chasing money. When I finally couldn't take that anymore and changed back to basketball, I felt happier. There was no money involved in it at first, so I had to get creative in order to stay in it. I became a teacher and tried these other things. No value that you can put on money compares to the value you gain when you have a passion for something. The people around you may not get it, but that's okay. There will always be negative people. It is the simplest thing to be. But it's one of life's little mysteries. You have to work to stay positive; you have to work to find the good. But I am back to that feeling of choosing the extraordinary. A life of just making money didn't make me feel extraordinary. Involving myself in a craft and process with others while trying to make a good living gives me that feeling.

I got the unique opportunity to work at a very prestigious law firm in Century City, just outside Beverly Hills, California. The building I worked in was the same one that appeared in the movie *Die Hard*. I arrived every morning when it was dark and left when it was dark. I had a long commute, so when I got home, I would go straight to bed because I had to wake up early to get on the infamous Southern California freeway system and sit in traffic.

I saw incredible wealth in the office. One of the partners had an entire aquarium wall of exotic fish; it was unreal. They had wine-and-cheese parties before noon just because they signed or closed a deal.

I found my work interesting. I read correspondences and got files for the associates, helping them with their respective cases. One day, when I got to an associate's office, I noticed he had spent the entire night in his office to prepare his case. He looked out of sorts and asked me why I wanted to do this when I could play basketball. I remember just looking out the window.

It was dark, and I, too, began thinking, *Why am I here? What am I looking for?* These guys had money, yet they weren't the happiest individuals I knew. It was at that point I realized this wasn't for me. I feel grateful that attorney advised me to pursue my passion in life.

Find what you feel passionate about, and then get creative. Modify, adjust, and adapt. Find a way to stay in it. Nothing great gets created without passion. We all inherently know this to be true, yet so much negativity still surrounds going after your dreams. I have often asked myself, *Why? Why do we do this after first telling young kids they can dream big and be anything they want?*

Most of the time, at least in my experience, when people don't fulfill their dreams in their youth, resentment comes. People don't want to be left behind. You know that. And I deal with the fact that you have to be grateful for the negative people too. Use those negative people as part of the fuel to keep you going as well. Say to yourself, *Thank you for the negativity that you're bringing because it has actually provided me with the fuel to move forward. It has given me more incentive to do what I'm doing.* You will find no greater satisfaction than when you prove negative people wrong. I'm not saying it's easy to ignore the naysayers. Of course, you get disappointed, and when you feel down, everybody wants to talk bad about what you do. And you can't make any money at your passion at first because society is based on nothing but financial gain and the status that comes with financial gain.

People who have helped me along the way have given me encouragement and inspiration, and other ones who have fought me with negativity have fueled me just as much if not more than the positive ones in some ways. I am driven by people who say I can't do something. They motivate me to have a razor-sharp focus, to understand that I can prove them wrong. I have those people in my life, who give me as much of a drive as anything else. It takes appreciation and gratitude to say, "Thank you for being that thorn in my side. Because of you, I'm driven to succeed."

Any endeavor that we undertake has risk involved, and too many people are afraid of risk of any kind. So they say to the risk-takers and the dreamers, "Have security. Have the thing that you can count on." But if you have a fallback, you will constantly rely on it. You will always go back to saying, "You know, this didn't work out, but I have this job or this backup."

In an earlier chapter, we talked about everybody wanting control, wanting approval, and wanting security. The risk that's involved with pursuing your dream is real. But there is no way around it. I tell basketball players all the time, "Let's be two feet, not one foot, in." It's like when you go to a swimming pool and you see someone who dips a toe in, saying, "Ooh, it's too cold." Of course, the water will be cold at first. But then you see the bold person, the one who dives right in. And then he or she is in there, having a good time while the toe dipper remains cautious.

There are primarily two ways to get motivated: by pain or by pleasure. Sometimes, you need the negative people to tell you you're a fool for pursuing your dreams. How many unbelievable things have people created despite others not getting their vision? I'm sure Apple and Google were created that way. One of my friends, who runs a successful company, remembers people telling him his product was cost-prohibitive, it didn't yet have a market, and he'd never get this thing off the ground. Well, now his product is revolutionizing his category. He had to have all that negativity along the way to fuel his success. I said in an early basketball interview, "You know, I'm not six foot eight." But I had a burning desire to refine what I did and get better at it every single minute of every day. And I pursued it religiously with passion. I eliminated distractions.

Today, we have a lot to distract us. So the word *decide* comes in. You have to decide what is important. The old Latin word for *decide* means "to cut off," so a person has to cut off everything else, and he or she can do that figuratively and literally. You have to cut off all other distractions; you have to cut off people who are certain kinds of negative. That's what the word *decide* means. The obstacles will come, and you will have to overcome them by modifying, adjusting, and adapting along the way. And then you'll get to that finish line, whatever that finish line is for you. When you get to the finish line, that won't be the end of it.

Steve Jobs is a perfect example. Once Apple was created, he remained focused on the creativity process and making things better. He had constant visions and dreams. The trick for any sport, any coach, or any player isn't focusing on not feeling great in the moment. It's the whole exploration that comes with that journey, with self-doubt at the beginning, hurdles to overcome, and the tremendous successes and the failures as well.

I often tell people to make a life chart. Finding out how far you've come and significant things you've had to overcome will give you tremendous pleasure, and putting it all down on paper will give you much greater perspective. You'll realize you really can survive anything because you already have. I started doing life charts years ago. I wanted to see where I stood in life overall and get perspective. I also tried to do what I call *magic moments*, where I looked at what I did, asking every day, "What great thing happened today?" Most of the time, it concerns your children, or it's relationship based. You'll have your success in business, but have an awareness of an event that made you super happy and gave you a chance to smile. Just reflect and remember it, and it puts a smile on your face all over again. We all have these little moments. They just get lost or buried in time. With a life chart, you may discover a lot more of those magic moments than you thought of originally.

A life chart provides a great clue that you are doing what you are meant to do. Sometimes, it's actually hard to know our calling. We might not even know our strengths when others find them quite obvious. Your true friends likely can tell you a little bit more about what you're good at.

But the best way to find your passion is to look at what you do when you have time off. What do you do with that time? Likely, you do what really moves you—that thing you would do even if no one paid you to do it. Joseph Campbell famously wrote, "Follow your bliss, and the money will come." Even better is the fact that when you follow your bliss, earning money will no longer be the most important thing.

So find what motivates you, and don't let anybody or anything convince you to do anything else. Life is too short to just get by.

Failure Is the Beginning of Your Comeback Story

Most people don't reach their dreams—but not because of failure. Most don't live their dreams because they give up. A lot of people give up at their first failure. Those who succeed don't stop at one failure; they don't stop at ten failures; they don't stop at a hundred, a thousand, or a million failures. They say, "This is my goal, and I will do whatever it takes to achieve it. I will learn the lessons from any failures. I will learn faster, work harder and smarter, and not quit until my dream is a reality." That's the difference between success and failure. Failure makes winners stronger. Failure makes winners hungrier. But it can make a lot of people give up. Winners don't enjoy failure. But they would never let failure stop them. The next time you encounter disappointment, you must remember that every great thing on this planet is here because the creator learned what did work but learned more about what did not work.

When we are kids, we don't stop at failure. When we first learn to ride a bike, we get knocked down time after time, but we get up and push forward until we achieve our goal of riding the bike. But then we get old, and most of us get weak. We come up with excuses as to why we don't get back on the bike. No—tell yourself the truth. Get back on the bike, learn why you failed, and make sure you don't fall again and you are stronger for having learned the lesson.

Failure is not the end of your story; it is the start of your comeback story. If our stories ended with letdowns, there would be no greats—greats like Jordan, Einstein, and Edison. If these people stopped trying, their greatness would not fill the world as it does today. Failure is nothing but a lesson and motivation to the winner. It is fuel. The difference between those who win and those who lose is that winners decide to find greater meaning in their setbacks. Let your defeats grow you; let them develop you. Failure is not the end; it's the start—the start of your comeback story.

The only way you can call something a failure is if you quit. If you keep going, it's only a hurdle—one you will overcome. Never quit. Keep pushing; you will get there in the end. Failure doesn't exist in a line of champions. It pushes them to a higher level. Are you a champion? Will you accept failure and keep going? Learn the lessons, apply the lessons, come out stronger than before, and keep going. Some people fear setbacks so much they never even try; they never even start. Some people give up right when they are about to succeed. They are so close when they throw in the towel—don't let that be you.

Thomas Edison didn't fail. He found one thousand ways that did not work. But he only needed one way that did work. As Einstein said, "Failure is success in progress." Keep going, and you will succeed. Use failure as fuel. Use it as motivation; it cannot defeat you in the long run. Use it to make you. Refuse to be defeated. Learn the lesson. Find a new path and a different way to your goal. There is always a way!

The final step on the path is to be grateful for everything, the positive and the negative, because both are motivators if you look at them the right way.

Pursue your passion. You will have ups and downs along the way, but I assure you you'll never regret the decision.

So in summary, here are the nine steps to living your dreams:

1. Make the decision to live an extraordinary life with no regrets.
2. Realize that many are on the journey with you to help you succeed.

3. Pay attention to the details, not just the end goal.
4. Know your craft, skill, or business so well that your confidence becomes unshakable.
5. Be willing to roll the dice and take chances.
6. Enjoy the ride.
7. Let go of needing complete control.
8. Be grateful for everything, the positive and the negative. Both can be great sources of fuel.
9. Don't be afraid of failure. Embrace it. Learn the lesson it gives you, and keep on going. You will get there in the end. Take your shot; make your play!

Printed in the United States
By Bookmasters